CLUTTER

AN UNTIDY HISTORY

CLUTTER

Jennifer Howard

AN UNTIDY HISTORY

Belt Publishing

Printed in the United States of America
First edition 2020
2 3 4 5 6 7 8 9

ISBN: 978-1-948742-72-6

Belt Publishing
3143 W. 33rd Street #6
Cleveland, Ohio 44109
www.beltpublishing.com

Cover by David Wilson
Book design by Meredith Pangrace

For Mark, Lela, and Finn—my organizing principle, always

Have nothing in your houses that you do not know to be useful or believe to be beautiful.

—William Morris, from "The Beauty of Life,"
a lecture given at the Birmingham Society
of Arts and School of Design, 1880

CONTENTS

PROLOGUE

In My Mother's House:
A Personal History of Clutter

'm sitting on the floor in my mother's house, surrounded by stuff.

It's everywhere—heaps and stacks and boxes and bags of it. Newspapers and junk mail sprawl across the living-room floor. Teacups hold hundreds of pennies and paper clips and rubber bands. A dozen lamps, shades off, fill the space under a harpsichord that hasn't been played in a decade.

I get up and make my way through the wreckage like a first responder assessing the damage after a hurricane. Each room presents a new scene of devastation. The coffee table in the living room is a shipwreck of mugs and glasses with brown sludge at the bottom. When I pick up one of the pizza boxes stacked next to it, crusts rattle like bones inside. Takeout Chinese food festers in Styrofoam clamshells nearby; I open one and discover the contents stinking, moving, crawling.

In the dining room, the scene of so many school-day breakfasts and holiday dinners, the table has become a graveyard of Tupperware containers and empty jars. On the screened-in porch, there's no room to walk between the bags stuffed with recycling and trash, the broken chairs and never-used roasting pans, the scratching posts for cats dead since the 1990s.

The kitchen is a health inspector's nightmare. Larvae squirm through the sludge that covers the dirty dishes filling the sink. Mouse droppings dot the countertops like sprinkles on a cupcake. When I open cabinets, I discover that the mice have gnawed into the stockpile of specialty flours and dry goods that haven't been touched in years. A small corpse, victim of one the poison trays my mother has cached all over the house, lies mummified in a corner.

Squalor and chaos have infiltrated every room—upstairs, downstairs, attic, basement. No space has been left untouched. In the bedrooms, impromptu pathways thread through corridors of books and bills and weave around piles of clothes and towels and linens. To reach the shelves in the spare room—my old bedroom—I have to scale mini-mountains of bagged junk and clamber over the bed, the one clear space left. I can't see the floor in my mother's office or the top of her desk. Every available surface, including the windowsills, has been taken over by detritus—pill bottles, nail scissors, binder clips, chopsticks, pens, pencils, coupons, pocket change, random keys, sticks of chewing gum.

This is how my mother has been living, and it has almost killed her. And now it is my problem to deal with.

As the initial disgust and horror begin to subside, the magnitude of the task ahead sinks in. The sheer amount of stuff staggers me. The closets in the bedrooms overflow with Amalfi and Ferragamo shoes, formal gowns from four decades of artistic galas and premieres, and pantsuits for the 1980s and '90s career woman, with boxy jackets and silk scarves and gold jewelry big enough to be noticed but not large enough to be garish. My mother's friends always used to compliment her taste, tell her how elegant and pulled-together she seemed. Those friends would have been shocked at how, in the months leading up to the current crisis, she took to wearing my late stepfather's oversized jeans and shirts, because she could not—or would not—do laundry for herself. At the bottom of the basement steps, I discover a mountain of dirty clothes, tossed down the stairs and left to fester.

I find emotional snares as well as mouse traps scattered throughout the house. My mother has been a mystery to me all my life, an unpredictable presence who made sure I was fed and clothed but otherwise hovered out of emotional reach. Now, as I excavate the ruins of her material life, I find clues, artifacts in situ that offer glimmers of who she might have been.

With an artist's eye, she gravitated to fine and expensive things. My mother shopped to make herself feel better, to feel she had value in the world, to feel love and to express it. She excelled at giving practical gifts. She used to say that you needed the best equipment for the job. Much of the clutter I have to dig through consists of the tools of her various trades. She can't use them now.

In my old bedroom, her library fills three walls of shelves. To browse the books I have to climb over archive boxes, bags stuffed with half-finished knitting projects, an old doll carriage, a sewing machine, shoeboxes that house the extensive collection her closets can't contain. I count 500 cookbooks at least, heavy on Mediterranean cuisines. Others speak to Mom's salt-of-the-earth side: books on how to pickle things, books of chutney recipes, books of local favorites from tiny New England towns. My mother used to buy cookbooks the way some people buy mystery novels or romances, always hungry for more even though she made only a handful of the recipes. Making new things wasn't the point. She hungered for the contemplation of lovely food served in elegant settings.

The contents of the other sets of shelves surprise me more. The Tolkiens and Le Guins and Lloyd Alexanders of my childhood have been displaced by a self-help library that catalogs attempts, over decades, to make sense of a disordered emotional life. Mom lived around the corner from a good public library but rarely went there to borrow something to read. Instead she propped up the self-help publishing industry seemingly by herself. She bought books on how to cope with being the adult child of an alcoholic, books on how to manage anger, books on how to make a marriage work, books on how to be a successful woman entrepreneur. Meanwhile her life, as I knew it, continued its unpredictable run: angry moods, marital strains, precarious finances. Finding her self-help library made me wonder if she'd possessed more self-knowledge than I knew.

If so, it was too little, too late.

———————

From what I know about my mother, the extreme clutter that imprisoned her was a crisis years in the making. Here's a working theory: The lacks and chaos of her childhood fed a lifelong compulsion to comfort herself with things. Clutter, like emotional chaos, has a way of running in families, passed down like curly hair or blue eyes or musical ability.

My mother's troubles with stuff began in Worcester, Massachusetts, where she grew up the oldest child of an alcoholic engineer and a housewife. She told me once that she and her younger brother and sister each got one pair of new shoes for the school year. No wonder she envied the purses and chic shoes of the wealthy girls from Shrewsbury Street. More than material things, however, she must have craved stability, something in short supply with an alcoholic father and passive, often critical mother. So she found an escape. She used her talents as a pianist and organ player to put Worcester behind her and secure a spot at Oberlin's conservatory.

As a child, I was in awe of my mother's creative side. I would go to sleep at night listening to her practice the Baroque intricacies of Bach and Scarlatti on the harpsichord, cascades of notes that flowed from her deft fingers. She painted, too, mostly still-life arrangements with velvet-dark backdrops against which flowers showed their best selves in vases. On the canvas and at the keyboard she found no room for disorder.

In her personal life, though, she increasingly trailed chaos in her wake. She married my father too young, under pressure from my grandmother, before she had settled on who she was and what she wanted. The marriage did not last; when I was five, my mother left my father. She always presented the departure to me as necessary for self-preservation, though it disordered my world in a way that reverberated through my childhood and beyond.

After the split, my mother went on to acquire two more husbands, a succession of irritating dogs, multiple harpsichords, hundreds of books and records, and more Italian shoes than anybody could have needed. She divorced her second husband and outlived the third. The shoes and the dogs she kept, along with almost every other possession she ever owned.

I'll never know whether my mother could have stopped acquiring and accumulating. All I know is that she could not or would not get rid of anything. Dementia, diagnosed late but creeping into her mind over a decade, must have amplified her hoarding tendencies, but she never could bear to get rid of things even when her mind was all her own. Clutter, built up over decades, paralyzed her long before the disease made it impossible for her to manage it.

Surely she knew that the mess she took years to create would someday be mine to clean up. Still she shopped, and the heaps and stacks and boxes and bags grew in number, and the livable space left to her shrank and shrank until there was almost none left, in a house too full of everything.

What happened to my mother is not altogether her fault, although it's hard to see that while standing amid the domestic rubble she left behind. Her story is a cautionary tale that illustrates an unpleasant truth about contemporary America: This culture creates a craving for things we don't really need, often to distract ourselves from what what's really missing—love, connection, meaningful work, a sense of something beyond the self, a care for the natural world that goes beyond exploiting it to make more stuff to buy and sell.

Americans learn from cradle to grave that stuff = happiness, and when the things we buy do no not make us happy, or when the buzz of the last purchase wears off, we buy more. And more, and more—whether it's fast fashion or cars or pet supplies or smartphones. The consumer engine burns through precious personal and environmental resources to feed desires that can never fully be satisfied. That's the point. If we felt we'd reached the point of material satiation, we'd stop shopping, and the engine would shut down.

Consumers' collective and inner lives suffer along with the planet. In *Notes on a Nervous Planet*, his book about anxiety, the novelist Matt Haig calls out "the physical clutter and mind debris of modern existence. He writes, "There is, in the current world, an excess of *everything*." The chaos of my mother's house, then, can be read as a microcosm of a much bigger mess. Countless others—daughters and sons, nieces and nephews, life partners and executors—deal with situations like mine every year. For my generation, it's practically a rite of passage, or at least a shared burden.

In search of distraction and some gentle guidance as I cut through the forest of my mother's belongings, I read Marie Kondo's bestseller *The Life-Changing Magic of Tidying Up*. When I pick up her book, Kondo has recently taken the country (or at least its lifestyle reporters and commenters) by storm—this mild-mannered Japanese organizing guru who, inspired in part by Shinto principles, advises readers to keep only those objects that "spark joy."

"Tidying up" doesn't begin to cover what happens when you clean fifty years' worth of detritus out of a family home, though. I find little to spark joy in dealing with my mother's mess, only the grim satisfaction of perseverance in the face of what seems an impossible task.

The book that comforts me most turns out to be Roz Chast's *Can't We Talk About Something More Pleasant?* Her 2014 illustrated memoir deals with her own parents' decline and "the massive, deeply weird, and heartbreaking job"—a perfect description—of having to sort through their stuff after they move out of their old apartment to an assisted-living facility. I wouldn't call it an uplifting read, but it makes my own situation feel less outlandish.

Eldercare woes, like miscarriages, turn out to be much more common than anybody tells you until they happen to you. As word gets out about my mother's crisis, friends come forward with their own stories of downsizing and caregiving, of financial and legal arrangements, of painful conversations, and—rare, precious, and enviable—of elder transitions that prove painless, even joyful, a liberation from stuff rather than a forced parting from it. These friends and I swap the names and numbers of caseworkers and personal organizers and junk haulers. I learn, too late, about social services that might have been able to rescue my mother from her domestic squalor before it set off a crisis.

Still, I drag the weight of my mother's belongings everywhere I go. Questions run through my head when I'm walking or driving, at work or at the gym, at my desk or at dinner. They wake me up at night. Where will it all go? What can be salvaged? What can I bear to throw away, and how do I separate treasures from trash when so much of it—so much stuff!—looks like trash?

At a certain point, existential concerns give way to practical ones. The only way to proceed is to begin. I fill and refill the trash and recycling bins. Out with the newspapers and magazines and junk mail. Out with the unused jam jars and the desiccated condiments. Off to a local charity with my late stepfather's clothes, left untended for the two years since his death.

The rest of his belongings will take longer; his children live far away and I can't bear to throw out his photos and family papers and heirlooms, so I send them off in batches. Documents take time to sort but ship easily. It turns out not to be so easy to transport a grandfather clock, chimes and all, across the country.

Unlike my mother, who fought off all offers of help until a crisis intervened, I am not convinced that I can handle it all myself. I recruit help in the form of a personal organizer, a quiet and efficient woman with the demeanor of a therapist and the discretion of a family retainer. She spends multiple days going through daunting stacks of paper and sifts out the important documents from years' worth of junk mail and newspapers.

As the paper forest diminishes, it becomes possible for me to see the beginnings of a path (literal and figurative) through all the stuff. Some people, meaning well, suggest I get rid of it all—just empty the house and sell it. Easier said than done.

All these things have been out of circulation for so long, but they could, some of them at least, be useful again. I cling to that hope, faint as it is. I become a hanging judge, ruthless, dispatching a parade of unfortunates to their doom. There's no joy but there is a savage pleasure in cleaning up messes that have sat untended for decades. My mother couldn't or wouldn't deal with them. I have to, so I do. I go through the house room by room. I cull and cull and cull again.

The volume of stuff staggers me. No matter how many bags of trash and recycling I move out, no matter how many

Goodwill runs I make, more stuff appears, rising up like a dead army. I joke, too often, that the best way to solve the problem would be with a can of gasoline and a match. In those moments, I wonder how much of any of our things we'd really miss.

Frank the junk hauler sees me through the worst of the culling. Frank and his crew make multiple trips to my mother's house over a number of months. Each time they arrive in a pink truck that holds more than I would have believed possible. The geometric precision with which they load the truck reminds me of the game Rush Hour, where the player has to maneuver a car through a traffic jam by moving other cars to create a space to slip through. Every inch counts.

It's easy to like Frank, with his cheerful manner and his quiet sympathy. He could be the brother I don't have. To take my mind off the pain of discarding, Frank tells me about stories about families he's worked with who can't stop fighting over things even as he's carrying them out of the house. Maybe, I think, I'm lucky I only have to fight with myself about what to salvage.

Even with the help of professionals, cleaning out my mother's house will take years, more nights and weekends and lunch hours and vacation days than I can tally. It would be a full-time job if I could take time away from my actual full-time job.

Instead I have to do it in bits and pieces. It eats into precious time I could be spending with my spouse, my children, my writing. I have never done anything this hard. I feel guilty and angry through much of it. It feels, over and over again, like I'm killing my mother and being undone by her at the same time. Unable to challenge her about it—dementia absolves its sufferers of responsibility for what they did before it took them—I confront a house full of proxies, the physical remnants of her personality and routines.

19

What can be hard to see, especially when you're in drowning in a cleanup, is that clutter is a luxurious problem to have. In many parts of the world, people don't wrestle with too many things; they have to figure out how to survive with too few. The minimalist slogan "Less stuff, more life" doesn't apply when life itself is at risk.

While I was occupied with the ruins of my mother's life, Europe was confronting a refugee crisis bigger than any since World War II. While I tried to figure out where Mom and all her things would go, migrant parents from Central America were trying to get themselves and their children to safety in the United States and being forcibly separated at the US-Mexico border. Later, while I worked on this book, devastating fires in California and Australia ate through homes and communities, ravaged ecosystems, and consumed the possessions of many lifetimes. As I finished it, a killer virus was wreaking pandemic havoc all over the world.

People desperate to escape violence, disease, natural disasters, or civil unrest are forced to confront existential questions about stuff. If you had to flee for your life, what would you take with you? What objects are truly irreplaceable?

My mother never answered that question. Instead she kept everything. She planned for yard sales and Goodwill runs that never happened. In a house with a basement, attic, and garage, she always found corners in which to stow the excess. She'd deal with her stuff when the right time came along.

It never did. For many people in this society, it never does.

I wanted to understand how people like my mother become prisoners of their things—and how clutter became a collective problem big enough to spawn bestsellers and reality TV shows. The hunt for answers eventually led me backward in time, to the Victorians and the onset of industrialism and mass production; and forward, to where the rise of consumer culture has led us and what we can do about it. But first I needed to understand more about how individuals' relationships with their things can slip—as it did for my mother—from consumerism into dysfunction, even pathology.

CHAPTER 1
Finder Keepers:
Hoarding Disorder and Shame

S trange as it feels to say this, my mother is lucky. In the most extreme cases, clutter can be crushing—literally. The volume of things socked away in my mother's modest 1930s Colonial shocked me. In the annals of extreme clutter and hoarding behaviors, her situation would barely rate a footnote.

The most infamous case I know of concerns Homer and Langley Collyer, brothers in New York City whose Harlem brownstone became, in the early decades of the twentieth century, a death trap of junk, including hundreds of thousands of newspapers. Writing in the *New York Times* in 2003, journalist Franz Lidz recalled his father's description of the premises: "Within the winding warrens were tattered toys and chipped chandeliers, broken baby carriages and smashed baby grands, crushed violins and cracked mantel clocks, moldering hope chests crammed with monogrammed linen."

It all came to a crashing end in 1947, when accumulated clutter collapsed on top of Langley and crushed him; Homer, blind and bedridden and dependent on his brother, starved to death. Nearly a century later, the brothers' story still stands as a cautionary tale for a cluttered age: Your stuff really might be the death of you.

———————

Hugs and all, the gentle interventions that Marie Kondo stages in her Netflix show represent a departure from how

American society has long treated people, like the Collyers, who let their stuff accumulate to the point of squalor. We have a long history of being obsessed with—and judging—people with hoarding disorder.

As I researched this book, I spent painful hours watching episodes of *Hoarders*, probably the best known of a crop of reality-TV shows that specialize in taking viewers on deep dives into the homes of people living with extreme clutter. *Hoarders* has been on the air for a decade now, a testament to how much we enjoy vicarious glimpses into other people's desperate domestic circumstances Each episode follows a team of organizers, junk haulers, and "extreme clutter" specialists as they confront people living in dangerous, squalid conditions.

The show's cameras swoop in on heaps of garbage and debris and zoom through labyrinths of stuff, documenting the wreckage as if it were a murder scene. Nerve-rattling music worthy of a horror movie increases the sense of dread about what's about to unfold. Concerned relatives and friends appear on camera, tearful and angry, to talk about the horrors they've observed and how worried they are. The intervention team takes turns confronting the afflicted individuals about their problem: *Can't you see this? You really think this is how you should be living? That smell isn't mold. It's feces!*

Etc. These are not gentle interventions but exercises in making private shames public, and they belong to a long tradition. Long before reality TV cameras invaded the private spaces of those who suffer from hoarding disorder, for instance, the media made hay out of the Collyer brothers, highly educated and eccentric scions of a well-to-do New York doctor and his opera-singer wife. The family moved into a Harlem brownstone in 1909 and amassed an impressive library of more than 25,000 books. The doctor and his wife sent their sons to Columbia University to study engineering

(Langley) and law (Homer). Langley also mastered the piano, even playing at Carnegie Hall.

Those gilded beginnings did not lead to fortunate lives. The brothers' parents died in the 1920s. By the spring of 1947, when the Harlem police got a tip that somebody had perished in the house, the brothers had become true recluses, with Homer blind and disabled and dependent on his brother to take care of him.

The brownstone contained so much stuff it took the police two hours to get inside. In the prologue to *Stuff: Compulsive Hoarding and the Meaning of Things*, a seminal series of case studies of people with hoarding disorder, researchers Randy O. Frost and Gail Steketee describe what the first responders found:

> Objects of every variety crammed the house—newspapers, tin cans, magazines, umbrellas, old stoves, pipes, books, and much more. A labyrinth of tunnels snaked through each room, with papers, boxes, car parts, and antique buggies lining the sides of the tunnels all the way to the ceiling. Some of the tunnels appeared to be dead ends, although closer inspection revealed them to be secret passageways. Some of the tunnels were booby-trapped to make noise or, worse, to collapse on an unsuspecting intruder.

The catalog of incredible objects kept growing as police spent the next few days searching what was, quite literally, a deathtrap. They found Homer's body quickly; it took almost three weeks to uncover Langley, only a few feet away. Homer had died of starvation. Langley had been crushed by one of his own booby-traps.

Having too many newspapers and magazines doesn't, on its own, signify pathology. Turning bales of newspapers into elaborate, booby-trapped fortifications takes the problem to the level of diagnosable hoarding disorder. The Collyers' stockpile strains the imagination, not just because of the tunnels and booby-traps it contained but because of the volume and variety of things they amassed: 170 tons of belongings, including 14 grand pianos and a Model T. How they got all that into the house in the first place remains a mystery.

The Collyers persist as a touchstone for discussions of extreme clutter and its consequences. But the stories about them didn't really have much to tell me about what it feels like to live with hoarding disorder. For that, I drove up to Philadelphia in June 2017 for a day-long conference organized by the Philadelphia Hoarding Task Force, a coalition of city agencies and nonprofit social-service groups who deal, in different ways, with extreme clutter on the residential front. Similar task forces, some more official and organized than others, have sprung up around the country in the last few years, as communities move away from forced cleanouts and search for alternative interventions that actually work.

The conference keynote speech, given by a man named Lee Shuer, gave a vivid account of what extreme clutters feels like when it belongs to you. Shuer, who struggled with hoarding disorder and now works with other sufferers, described a visit he made to the former site of the Collyer brothers' house in New York City.

Reality-TV cameras capture clutter but not the person behind it. "It's painful when you actually know the story behind the story," Shuer said. "That's what we're missing with a show like *Hoarders*."

Shuer urged the audience to look beyond the spectacle to the humans at the center of it. Headlines at the time played up the sensational side of the Collyers' situation, the magnitude of their hoard, the dismal ending of their story. Those lurid details have kept the brothers alive in the popular imagination. People forget they possessed brilliant minds, with talents for engineering and medicine and music.

"Look at what they were dealing with," Shuer said. "What they were dealing with was a lifetime of trauma, of being afraid of the world, and barricading themselves in."

Shuer's own experience defies the hoarding stereotypes that pop culture perpetuates. He wasn't a shut-in or afflicted with dementia; he handled adult responsibilities. He had roommates, a job, a girlfriend. He also had a problem—hoarding disorder—that threatened the good things in his life. Unlike the Collyers, Shuer got a happy ending. He and his now-wife, Bec Belofsky Shuer, worked together on his recovery, and have since gone on to become advocates for those with hoarding disorder.

What jumped out at me from Shuer's talk was how much harm the casual use of terms like "hoarder" can inflict. To label someone a hoarder reduces the person to the problem.

The self-descriptions of people with hoarding disorder evoke a startlingly different vision of what the world condemns as a personal failing. Shuer listed some alternative labels: *finder-keeper, collector, historian, artist.*

It took me aback at first to hear such positive terms used to describe individuals whose behaviors are routinely (and often understandably) stigmatized as abnormal, unhealthy, disgraceful, or dangerous. If you have lived through wrangling another person's extreme clutter, such relabeling isn't easy to embrace. I saw very little artistry at work in my mother's mess. Renaming a problem does not make it go away.

Then again, as I learned in Philadelphia, research and experience indicate that kindness works better than shame in getting clutter victims the help they need. In the final session of the Philadelphia conference, Bec Shuer talked about what it was like to be close to someone with hoarding disorder. She offered this: "People with too much stuff are people with good intentions. They're artists, they're environmentalists, they're historians. Don't forget that there's a person in the room with all those boxes and bins."

I thought of the dozens and dozens of shoeboxes in my mother's closet. Was she just an enthusiastic appreciator and collector of fine footwear, or a damaged personality who used a taste for high-end Italian pumps and flats to dull the sting of old hurts? She's not able to answer that question now, and would have resisted it even before dementia took over. But my asking it, even without hope of a conclusive answer, sets loose a compassionate spirit I had a hard time summoning when I was in the throes of the cleanout.

A conversation with Dr. Gregory S. Chasson, associate professor of psychology and director of clinical training at the Illinois Institute of Technology, helped me understand why the choice of terms matters. "A lot of people with hoarding tendencies view their objects as an extension of themselves," he told me. Call somebody a hoarder, call their possessions junk, and you might as well be calling them trash.

No wonder those who struggle with hoarding behaviors often resist treatment, according to Chasson, who's thought a lot about the social and economic costs of extreme clutter. "The stigma is pretty high. It's on a par with the stigma associated with severe mental illness," he says. "People want to distance themselves from people with hoarding."

Chasson's research includes work on how pop-cultural representations of hoarding amplify the powerful sense of shame it generates. He endorses the need for more sensitive terminology. Terms like "finder-keeper" and "object attachment disorder" don't wound the way "hoarder" and "hoarding" do.

The potential for shame makes people less likely to ask for help until they find themselves under duress—confronted with eviction, for instance. "It's a pretty difficult problem to treat," Chasson says. Drastic, late-stage interventions also eat up a lot of municipal resources. "This really costs the public quite a bit of money," he says.

You can't pop a pill and be magically cured of hoarding behaviors, but individual cognitive behavioral therapy holds promise, Chasson says. So does peer-led group counseling. The Shuers run workshops, called "Buried in Treasures," that follow a therapeutic model developed by David Tolin, Randy Frost, and Gail Steketee, three researchers who have led the way in recent years in learning more about hoarding disorder and related behaviors and how to treat them.

The "Buried in Treasures" approach encourages participants to uncover what drives their hoarding. For instance, individuals who accumulate extreme clutter may value it because it makes them feel safe, or because it compensates for a trauma they've experienced.

To see clutter as an expression of pain recasts the reveal-and-shame attitude popularized in news stories and reality TV shows. As Shuer said at the Philadelphia conference, for someone with hoarding disorder, the essential question isn't "How did you let it get to this?" but "What pain are we trying to handle? How do we figure out where that pain is coming from and how we decide to deal with it?"

Did my mother suffer from clinical diagnosable hoarding disorder? I will never know. Until recently, the mental-health profession wasn't well equipped to make such a diagnosis anyway; most providers didn't recognize it as a condition separate from Obsessive Compulsive Disorder (OCD) or anxiety disorders.

While popular culture continued to be obsessed with and reinforce taboos against hoarding, the mental health profession largely ignored it. As recently as 2010, when Frost and Steketee published *Stuff*, many therapists and psychiatrists still filed hoarding disorder under the broad label of OCD.

In the book, Frost recounts how he stumbled on hoarding as a fruitful area of research when, in the 1990s, one of his students at Smith College pointed out how few studies existed on the subject. That eventually led, in 1993, to an article in the journal *Behavior Research and Theory* based on a series of home visits with "chronic savers" (another less shameful term). They shared certain traits: They were "perfectionistic and indecisive, having trouble processing information quickly enough to feel comfortable making decisions."

These field insights helped open the way for the recognition of clutter as a symptom of something other than OCD. In 2013, three years after *Stuff* came out, hoarding disorder was at last recognized as a distinct mental disorder: The American Psychiatric Association's influential *Diagnostic and Statistical Manual of Mental Disorders*, Fifth Edition (*DSM-5*)—the diagnostic bible for the mental-health profession—brought the condition out of the shadows and identified it as a clinically diagnosable problem. In its extreme form, the disorder affects a significant number of people in the United States: The APA estimates that between 2 and 6 percent of the US population suffers from it.

"Chances are you know someone with a hoarding problem," Frost and Steketee write. Diagnosed or not, your parent or grandparent, your nephew or your first cousin once removed might be afflicted. It's not rare—just rarely acknowledged.

Frost and Steketee developed a theory about why that is: Hoarding takes place in private spaces, out of sight, which makes it "an 'underground' psychopathology." Clinically, it shares some symptoms with impulse-control disorders (ICDs), which partly explains why it was lumped in with OCD for so long.

Curiously, though, where OCD puts anxiety front and center, hoarding can be driven by "a mixture of pleasure and pain." One can take pleasure in the acquisition of things and feel pain because of an inability to manage or get rid of the resulting overabundance of stuff.

I wondered whether extreme clutter afflicts certain socioeconomic and demographic groups disproportionately. Does it affect all genders more or less equally? (Women tend to live longer, which gives us more time to accumulate.) Is clutter a disease of affluence—more money, more things? Is it a response to deprivation? (We've all heard that truism about how people who grew up during the Depression hang on to everything, though I have yet to find hard evidence that backs up that theory.)

I asked Gregory Chasson, who in addition to his academic work and research serves as the co-executive director of the Chicagoland Hoarding Task Force. "You're going to see all walks of life experience this," he said. "It's pretty egalitarian."

In his experience, the struggle with stuff afflicts people with a lot of money and people with very little. Clutter trouble crops up at every income level and among diverse demographic groups. It's not a black, white, Latino, or Asian problem, a male or female problem, a rich person's or poor person's problem. It's *everybody's* problem.

Given all that, communities ought to have robust systems and resources in place to deal with it. The system hasn't caught up to the need for help, in part because individuals tend to keep their struggles with clutter hidden for fear of being shamed or even evicted. Friends and family members who want to help often don't know how to do so constructively.

My mother, once sociable, stopped inviting friends over as her house got worse and worse. Most of them had no clue about how bad her situation got in her last years living there. Later, too late, I realized I could have made an anonymous call to the local department on aging and asked them to stage an intervention. I might not even have made that call if I had known it was an option. It would have come at a steep emotional cost.

Humane, workable solutions and interventions remain too hard to find. In recent years, hoarding task forces—like the one Chasson helps run in the Chicago area—have been formed to try to fill some of the gaps. They coordinate services and interventions offered by city agencies, first responders, clinicians, and social workers.

It's better than nothing, but it's an imperfect solution. Protocols differ jurisdiction by jurisdiction, Chasson says, which means that one locality might deploy different set of interventions than the town or county next door. That can complicate attempts to coordinate a regional response or establish best practices among different agencies, nonprofits, and individuals all trying to tackle the problem in their own ways. "Task forces really should be used to set up a more static system to help localities deal with these situations," Chasson says.

The Collyers represent extreme clutter at its most pathological, but someone doesn't have to suffer from hoarding disorder to have a real problem with clutter. A therapist described clutter to me as "delayed decisions," a phrase that neatly sums up that sense of overwhelm and paralysis that sets in when people cannot or will not deal with what they've accumulated.

Such delays can be deadly. As first responders know, clutter can kill people—both firefighters and those they're trying to save. The United States doesn't currently have reliable statistics on how many people die every year in clutter-related fires, according to Capt. Andrew Brown of the Philadelphia Fire Department (PFD). But Brown's conversations with fire marshals in the Philadelphia area and around the country turn up the same rough estimate: that 20 to 25 percent of civilian fire deaths involve clutter.

The PFD coined a term for extreme clutter: "heavy contents." It's a good phrase, neutral but evocative. It conjures up images of blocked exits and rooms so packed with stuff they're impassable. More important, it signals to first responders they're about to enter a situation packed with potential dangers. Brown applies a straightforward standard: Heavy contents mean a space has gotten so full it can't be used for its intended purpose.

Thanks in part to Brown, the PFD's incident-reporting database recently added the term to its list of factors that contributed to fires it responded to. Eventually, he hopes, that will generate more robust data and enable the department to get a better numerical handle on just how big the problem is.

I first heard Brown talk about clutter and first responders at the Philadelphia hoarding task-force conference. In December 2019, I drove up back up to meet him at the firehouse where he's stationed in southwest Philadelphia. Engine Company 40 serves a low-income area of rowhouses and junkyards—hence their nickname, the Junkyard Dogs.

In the station's watch office, the squad keeps a printout with a running list of dangerous properties. I read through the list of thirty or so addresses; nearly half were marked as hoarding situations. Brown estimates there's at least one heavy-contents house on every block in the neighborhood. Every station in the city maintains a similar list, he says.

Over toasted-cheese sandwiches blackened on the stationhouse grill, I heard stories about what it's like to enter an active fire scene. If there's smoke, the visibility is zero, which means navigating a scene by feel—*here's an armchair, that's a doorway.*

I tried to imagine a firefighter, loaded with 90 pounds of gear and tipping the scales at 250, going blind into a Collyer-like warren of stacked newspapers, books, boxes, garbage bags, furniture, and whatever else the occupant has saved over the years. They'd be carrying a hose full of water under high pressure—not an easy thing to navigate up and over and around obstacles. But that hose is a lifeline, vital to putting out the fire at its source and to guiding firefighters out safely again.

In a heavy-contents situation, water becomes both enemy and ally. It puts out fires. But pump hundreds of gallons of it onto masses of material and that stuff will get heavy fast. Floors can collapse under the weight of water-soaked clutter.

Firefighters move fast. So does fire. It can smolder undetected beneath stacks of papers, boxes, and other clutter, only to burst into open flames as soon as air reaches it. An observation Brown made at the hoarding conference stuck with me: *A house on fire is a house under demolition.*

That doesn't deter firefighters. A lot of them are ex-military and/or come from firefighting families. They stay in shape. They run toward danger when most of us would run the other way. But even a fit and fearless first responder can be tripped up or killed by heavy contents. An oxygen tank that under ideal conditions holds 30 or 60 minutes' worth of air runs out fast when someone is working at peak physical capacity. Every minute could mean the difference between life and death for firefighters and for the people they're there to help.

Brown points out that extreme clutter presents a real threat to health and safety even when there is no active fire to deal with. If EMTs don't have room to maneuver equipment or administer CPR, they can't help someone in medical distress.

Heavy contents can be expensive for the city, too. For instance, if a firefighter suffers even a minor injury—like a sprained ankle—because of extreme clutter, that means time spent on the injured list, and time-and-a-half paid to whoever fills in. And if health inspectors decide that a property has to be forcibly cleaned out, that costs the city about $10,000, according to Brown.

Behind every heavy-contents situation lies a personal story, a set of circumstances that has led someone into danger. Brown understands this at the personal level. His own experience with anxiety disorders—he has OCD—made it easier for him to understand what lies behind the inability to let things go, whether or not full-blown hoarding disorder plays a role. His late mother-in-law had what he thinks was an undiagnosed hoarding disorder. She piled up stuff as a defense, to the point where she couldn't use whole rooms.

I recognized some of the warning behaviors he described, because my mother did them too: She refused offers of help, kept visitors out of the house, "churned" stacks of paper— meaning that she would reshuffle them and feel like she had dealt with them.

His in-law's experience, combined with the realization that he or someone like him could be killed trying to do their jobs under such conditions, got Brown interested in how first responders ought to deal with heavy contents. He helped establish the Philadelphia Hoarding Task Force and the PFD's heavy-contents working group.

From a first responder's point of view, the time to help someone get heavy contents under control is *before* an emergency strikes—before the situation requires a "box run," which means the engine and hook-and-ladder trucks get called in. ("Box" is a holdover from the days of actual fireboxes.)

If it's a "shoe run"—the name for, say, a medical-distress call that doesn't require fire engines and firefighters suited up in uniform boots and gear—sometimes the responders can spot a dangerously cluttered situation. They might be able to make safety interventions on the spot, like clearing an exit or entrance, or they can alert an array of city agencies and social services that help is needed.

Forced cleanouts should be a last resort. What works best is not to shame someone for too much clutter but to point out the need to make changes for safety's sake. "I'm not telling you the same thing the rest of the world has told you for decades—that you have too much stuff," Brown told the hoarding conference audience. "I'm just telling you that you could be safer."

Brown has found it helps to describe what firefighters have to do when they respond to a fire. He might explain that the Philadelphia city code requires dwellings to have an "egress path" 36 inches wide—enough clearance for first responders to get in and occupants to get out. Safety goals come first: have clear stairs and access to utilities, eliminate tripping hazards, keep smoke alarms in working order.

Sending in a crew to clear everything out takes care of the immediate situation but does not work in the long term. "You can't just take somebody's life and throw it in the dumpster," Brown says.

Municipal and familial responses to extreme clutter have long focused on dealing with the immediate problem. Clean out the house: Problem solved. But forced clean-outs create fresh trauma for someone with hoarding disorder.

At the Philadelphia hoarding conference, Dr. Jennifer Sampson, a licensed family therapist, described how the physiological effects of a forced cleanout mimic those of a natural disaster like a hurricane or flood. Such events can trigger a phenomenon called Diffuse Physiological Arousal (DPA), with symptoms like rapid breathing and highly emotional behavior. Poor decision-making, substance abuse, and depression can set in.

If too much clutter poses a threat to human health and well-being, so does thoughtless intervention. "We wouldn't expect someone who's just lose their home to a hurricane to bounce back two days later," Sampson said. "We can't expect someone who's just gone through a hoarding clean-out to either."

That's a revolutionary insight in a culture with a long tradition of shaming people who can't keep their possessions under control. It makes me hopeful that society's collective response to hoarding disorder will shift away from the kneejerk impulse to stigmatize those afflicted. We'd be better off using that energy to examine the origins of our own vexed relationships with things.

CHAPTER 2

Material World:
The Victorian Roots of
Consumer Culture

Over the last couple of years, whenever the subject of this book came up, the conversation usually went in one of two directions. The person I was talking to would either share their own story about having to clean out a relative's stuffed-to-the-rafters place, or they would make a joke: "Want to come do some research at my house?"

Very few people I know feel in full control of their photos, clothes, toys, books, papers, or inboxes. We are individually and collectively overwhelmed.

Take a deep breath and listen to me: *It isn't our fault.*

The roots of this collective clutter agita stretch back in time, beyond individual choices and failings. The real blame lies with a system that ramped up production and delivery systems to provide an endless supply of material goods. That abundance, enviable in some ways, has become a trap. Once their basic needs—food, clothing, shelter—have been satisfied, modern consumers still default to acquisition mode.

It's a lot easier to buy than to discard. Consumer society exploits a phenomenon called the endowment effect: To own something imbues it with more value, almost as if the object were an extension of its owner. No wonder people struggle with letting go of stuff.

Add to this the mind-shredding distraction of living in a world awash in information, much of it negative, delivered round the clock via a multitude of devices, channels, and platforms. We're distracted, we're overwhelmed, we're existentially anxious about the state of a warming world beset by violence against humans and nature.

No wonder so many people cling to their belongings, and spend an inordinate amount of time organizing and managing them. No wonder organizing gurus who promise a more harmonious relationship with the essence of our material lives become bestsellers. I read the phenomenon as part of a collective self-soothing in the face of what feels like overwhelming chaos.

Some of the technologies that feed this cycle of consumption amid chaos haven't been around long. The origins of peak clutter, though, and the resulting fascination with people who promise to help cut through it, date back centuries. There isn't a Point Zero for the modern phenomenon of clutter. But the history of commerce and industrialization offer useful clues. Contemporary consumers live daily with the consequences of an appetite for stuff, a habit of acquisition, that goes back at least as far as the beginnings of the Industrial Revolution.

In other words, let's blame the Victorians.

———————

American domestic life circa 2020 feels far removed from that of the 19th-century Londoner or Liverpudlian. But Victorian notions of décor and comfort crossed the Atlantic and held sway in stateside imaginations and homes long after the age itself had faded into history books and period pieces on TV.

Since then, Victorian material culture has been stamped on the psyches of modern readers and viewers. Its staying power owes a debt to the 19th-century novelists and journalists who documented the era's tastes and excesses, and to the movie and TV producers who have kept alive those sometimes overheated but rich descriptions.

"Victorian" has persisted as a convenient if imprecise shorthand for a style that's heavy in every sense. "Victorian decor" invokes curtains-drawn houses where light goes to die and where rooms are filled with furniture dark, heavy, and overstuffed. Victorian rooms, as we imagine them, were temples (or mausoleums) of *things*, with every surface—mantels, tabletops, shelves, sideboards—obscured by ceramic figurines and keepsakes, and every inch of wall covered with paintings and portraits.

In 19th-century Britain, during Queen Victoria's rule, industrialization, urbanization, and the expansion of empire, together with an uptick in disposable income, put more objects within reach of more people. Mainstream conventions did not encourage those with means to be minimalists.

The burdens imposed by bourgeois domesticity were not lost on contemporaries. "It is a folly to suppose, when a man amasses a quantity of furniture, that it belongs to him. On the contrary, it is he who belongs to his furniture," wrote a wag in an 1854 squib on "The Tyranny of Furniture" in the satirical magazine *Punch*.

One of *Punch*'s best-known cartoonists and illustrators, Edward Linley Sambourne, and his wife, Marion, occupied a house at 18 Stafford Terrace in London's Kensington and Chelsea Borough. They moved in as newlyweds in the 1870s and lived there until their deaths four decades later. Preserved as a museum, 18 Stafford Terrace stands as a temple of well-appointed late-Victorian comfort, most of its original objects still in situ. Marion's diaries chronicle the life of the house and keep a running list of its contents, including more than 550 pieces of furniture. Her art- and furniture-loving husband spent a lifetime adding to the domestic load. The museum website suggests his acquisitive tendencies caused his spouse agitation: The master of the house attended auctions and sales until he died, a habit that added "ever more objects to the interiors, often to Marion's despair."

One detail, plucked from Marion Sambourne's diaries by Shirley Nicholson for her book *A Victorian Household*, staggers me: The family owned 66 upright chairs. Many were used in the dining room and drawing room, as one would expect, but 10 found their way to the master bedroom and another 10 more occupied the day-nursery.

This apparently wasn't considered over the top for the time. Although contemporaries did comment on the Sambournes' vast art collection, Nicholson observes, "contemporary drawings and photographs of other interiors show that most homes were just as crowded with furniture and miscellaneous *objects d'art.*"

In her book *Inside the Victorian Home*, historian Judith Flanders goes through a typical bourgeois dwelling room by room and examines the material goods likely to be found in each. She describes "the ever-increasing number of objects" in British homes of the era, especially from the 1860s on, which created a "deluge of 'things.'"

One description jumped out at me: "There were things to cover things, things to hold other things, things that were representations of yet more things." Things to hold other things: a prefiguring of the organization of life in the age of the Container Store.

The Victorian era helped establish expectations that persist today about what a well-appointed home looks like. Those standards drew on and accelerated the global circulation of resources, and promoted development of industries that turned those resources into consumer goods, not to mention the advertising and marketing systems that helped whet consumer appetites.

Although I'm focusing here on Victorian Britain, Western cultures and nations have never had a monopoly on consumerism. In his book *Empire of Things: How We Became a World of Consumers, from the Fifteenth Century to the Twenty-First*, the historian Frank Trentmann details the astonishingly complex and world-spanning systems of trade and exchange, extraction and production that evolved over the last half-millennium. A professor of history at the University of London's Birkbeck College, Trentmann directed the globally focused Cultures of Consumption research project from 2002-07. *Empire of Things* makes it abundantly clear, over 800 well-stuffed pages, how the history of consumerism extends far beyond the Euro-American context I grew up in and that shaped my own family's keep-everything attitude toward possessions. Renaissance Italy experienced a boom in conspicuous consumption when it came to personal attire and household furnishings. So did late Ming China, where the wife of a newly rich silk merchant might be seen sporting hairpin shaped like a phoenix, an ornament traditionally worn only by royal ladies. "Excess knew no limits, and there are some striking parallels between extravagance in late Ming and early Qing China and that recorded in Europe," Trentmann writes.

Conspicuous consumption has been around for hundreds if not thousands of years, though the phrase didn't arrive until the sociologist Thorsten Veblen coined it for his influential 1899 book, *The Theory of the Leisure Class*. In the 17th and 18th centuries, Trentmann observes, Britain and the Netherlands stepped up the game and "created a new kind of consumer culture" that offered more of almost everything: "The exponential rise in stuff went hand in hand with a rise in novelty, variety and availability, and this was connected to a more general openness to the world of goods and its contribution to the individual self, to social order and economic development."

In the 19th century, this trend accelerated not just in Britain but in many quarters of the world. Trentmann teases out complex interchanges among Europe, Asia, Africa, and the Americas. Goods and fashions circulated and took on new meanings, depending on the location, class, race, and relative status of producers and consumers. By 1776, Adam Smith could declare consumption to be "the sole end of all production"—an attitude that will probably feel familiar, if increasingly uncomfortable, to those who came into their own as citizen-consumers in the latter part of the 20th century.

I find echoes of this growing global hunger to consume in the attitudes that shaped the consumer habits and mindset I grew up with, a mindset that fundamentally influenced my mother's attitude toward her things—and set her up to be overwhelmed at last by them. In her house there is—was—a china press made from dark-stained solid wood. If a piece of furniture could brood, that one would. It stood in the same corner of the dining room since my childhood, holding a collection of seemingly useless items that would have been right at home in the dimly lit Victorian spaces of my imagination. It wasn't until I had to get rid of them that I really wondered where all those odds and ends came from.

What I see now is a trail of household goods that stretches back in time and across oceans, back to the Victorians and a mercantile society that came of age under the queen who gave the era her name. That society kept its financial and administrative brain in London and its beating industrial heart in cities like Manchester and Liverpool, drawing raw materials from and selling goods back to its far-flung empire.

Think of it this way: More people made more money in a society that put large amounts of resources into producing things better, faster, and in bigger quantities, and that concentrated its formidable market energies on urban centers where an empire's worth of stuff was for sale. Queen Victoria presided over the expansion of this system, but it pre-dated and survived her.

Lucy Worsley, author of *If These Walls Could Talk: An Intimate History of the Home*, offers up more evidence that the Victorians bear some responsibility for creating the conditions and the appetite for what became a glut of things. "Victorian living rooms contained more *stuff* than ever before," Worsley writes. Those affluent enough "wished to display the fruits of their industry and their empire. The Great Exhibition of 1851 inspired people to bring the whole world into their living rooms." The housekeepers must have been busy in the homes of the Sambournes and their well-heeled peers.

The centerpiece of the Great Exhibition was the Crystal Palace, a barrel-vaulted, steel-and-glass edifice big enough to house the world's wares—the ultimate china press. In his whimsical book *Victorian Things*, historian Asa Briggs breaks the Crystal Palace down into its components in order to convey a sense of just how overpowering the whole thing was. How big? The Crystal Palace, Briggs writes, "with its 293,655 panes of glass, its 330 standardized iron columns and its 24 miles of guttering, was the biggest and most extravagant of all the things on display, not just a building to house exhibits but in itself a symbol."

The Crystal Palace and its displays of material wonders inspired Victorians—the expanded classes with means, anyway—to spend some of those means on material goods just because they could. But it was hardly the first flush of what Worsley calls "this craze to possess." That fever flared up in the British body politic more than 150 years earlier, with the rise of imperial, commercial, and domestic systems set up to increase the trade in (and profit from) goods of all kinds.

"The late seventeenth-century invention of shops and shopping by an urban middle class who lived by trade was mirrored by the growth of a new type of domestic space,"

Worsley writes. "What might be termed the 'middle-class' living room was full of superfluous objects, chosen for ornament rather than use yet cheap and not truly beautiful: a barricade of possessions intended to stabilize a precarious position in the world."

In *Empire of Things,* Frank Trentmann examines the Crystal Palace not as a singular, gigantic cabinet of wonders but as one node in the vast network of commerce behind consumerism. The Grand Exposition, along with the Exposition Universelle in Paris and subsequent expos in many countries, "displayed the products of the world in a way that blurred the lines between culture and commodity."

That model of consumptive display carried over to the department stores of the late 19th century and the first half of the 20th. My mother spent countless hours at Lord & Taylor and Bloomingdale's; they were *destinations* for her, oases in which to spend money and relax and dream of the life she wanted to live—or escape whatever troubles plagued her in the here and now.

Department stores, like museums before them, offered generations of visitors/consumers like my mother a chance to "behold the world as a collection of goods, carefully displayed under glass." But they also held out the opportunity to bring the world's goods home. They were, Trentmann says, "self-conscious global institutions in ways not seen before, working in tandem with those other forces of globalization at the time: the world exhibition, the steamship, the postal service and migration."

Did Victorians ever feel the urge to purge some of excess? Did they go on decluttering sprees? I asked someone who digs up the things they threw away.

Tom Licence is a professor of medieval history and consumer culture at the University of East Anglia in the UK. A particular passion of his interested me, one that dates back to his boyhood, when his parents sent him bottle-hunting in pits of Victorian garbage (or rubbish, if you live in the UK). "Garbologist" would be a trendy and imprecise description for what he does.

Some of Licence's is the author of *What the Victorians Threw Away,* and the driving force behind the ongoing research project of the same name. He leads excavations of Victorian rubbish dumps that have become time capsules of the households that used them or, as he says in his book, "uniquely intimate deposits of information about past people's lives." "Their stories must be dug from the ground because everyday minutiae rarely appear in history books," he writes. "And they all contribute to the bigger story of how our great grandparents built a throwaway society from the twin foundations of packaging and mass consumption. To view this society through its rubbish is to learn how our own throwaway habits were forming."

That sounded promising as far as my theory of the Victorian origins of clutter went. "The Victorians certainly had a thing for what we might call 'clutter'" (while de-cluttering their lives in other ways)," Licence told me when I got in touch with him to hear more about his work. He confirmed that many Victorians, at least those who could afford it, did love their stuff. My early "Masterpiece Theatre" impressions of what "Victorian" meant weren't entirely off the mark.

"If you for example look at photographs of working-class and lower-middle-class parlors, you see a lot of clutter— mantelpiece cluttered with lots of ornaments, sideboard with lots of ornaments," Licence says. "I suspect they would have regarded it as a sign of opulence. One of the ideas behind having all these objects, it's about aping your social superiors.

And it's a sign of wealth and prosperity."

Decorative objects could also signal that their possessors had the wherewithal to indulge in recreational pursuits, like money to spend on a trip to the seaside. The late 19th century saw "the rise of leisure, with people taking more time off and visiting what we might call tourist attractions," Licence says. "That concept of leisure generates a whole category of objects."

A family jaunt to an English seaside town like Yarmouth or Blackpool often included a souvenir, a precursor of the miniature lighthouses and blown-glass sea creatures my children used to persuade me to buy, along with boxes of saltwater taffy, at the souvenir shops we visited during summer vacations at the Outer Banks of North Carolina. Then as now, "people go on holiday to the seaside and get a vase and put it on the mantelpiece," Licence says.

Some of Licence's rubbish explorations have focused on the Victorian town dump in the seaside resort town of Great Yarmouth, a tourist draw on the eastern coast of England, at the mouth of the River Yare. It was a popular destination then as now; Victorian summer tourists doubled the population from about 50,000 to 100,000. Those warm-weather visitors supported a souvenir trade whose remnants populate the dump.

"There's quite a lot of tourist kitsch, because the rubbish was mostly cleared up from the streets, hotels and seafront," Licence says. Visitors left behind all manner of things, including what he calls "portable tourist material culture items" (think travel shaving brushes) and souvenirs that catered to the tourist trade.

It's fascinating to browse the online database Licence and his team maintain of their finds. A shell-pink egg cup fragment dating to 1898 shows the Great Yarmouth town hall, painted or stamped on a gold-rimmed white oval. In the foreground, one can see the masts of ships anchored in the harbor, a reminder that Yarmouth was not only a beach town but a port city as well. Another souvenir cup from the tail end of the 19th century portrays Yarmouth beach from the jetty; tiny figures dot the sand, taking a dip or enjoying the view. The cup holds out an implicit promise to potential buyers: Buy it and hold onto the memories of strolling the strand. Such items should carry warnings, too: Accumulate enough souvenirs and your memories will get lost in the clutter.

The broken discards unearthed at the Yarmouth excavation also hint at how global the souvenir trade had become by the end of the 19th century, a prefiguring of today's "Made in China" cavalcade of disposable mementoes. The ceramic cups described by Licence's team came from Northern Europe and did not originate anywhere near the place they were designed to commemorate.

"Funnily enough, these Yarmouth souvenirs were made in Germany, then shipped over the North Sea to be sold on Yarmouth seafront," Licence says. "There are also exotic shells in the rubbish, which must have been imported from Africa and sold on the sea front as souvenirs (much as shells are sold in seaside boutiques today). You'll find also a number of broken statues and statuettes." Such material remains provide "more evidence of the clutter which to the Victorians signified wealth, comfort and opulence," he says.

Today's beachgoers in Yarmouth or Corolla would probably skip the egg cups, wherever they were manufactured, in favor of a snow globe or a refrigerator magnet. They might opt to bring home a tiny handful of the beach itself. "The Victorians also liked to bring home little bottles of sand," Licence says.

That detail in particular stuck with me: the hunger for palpable souvenirs, tangible reminder of places visited, that 21st-century vacationers share with the 19th-century pleasure-seekers. One of the items in my own house that's dearest to me is a soda bottle from Crete, filled with pebbles and stopped with a cork, which I filled there and brought home from a trip I made there with my father when I was 11 years old. (I don't remember what flavor the soda was.) There's a sailing ship embossed on the bottle, and it makes me think of far-flung shoals and the heroes of ancient stories sailing off on epic adventures. Mixed in with the pebbles are memories of the sandcastle my dad and I built on the beach, the flute-maker who tried to show me how to play, and a day at the Minotaur's home, the Minoan palace of Knossos, with its bare-breasted women and wave patterns on the walls. Maybe I am, at heart, a Victorian after all.

Souvenir—derived from the French verb meaning "to remember"—captures the Victorians' attitude toward such objects. "This is an age that's very caught up in memory," says Licence of the Victorian era. Sometimes souvenirs do live up to the name and earn the space they occupy. Most, though, become so familiar over time that lose their status as keepers of memory and become part of the burden of stuff that weighs down their owners rather than keeping the past alive. My heart goes out to the housekeepers of the past who must have watched with dismay as vacation memories faded but the objects still sat there to collect dust on mantels and shelves.

Even as Victorians experimented with new ways to capture people and places to be remembered—photography for instance—objects continued to serve as memory-keepers in a deeper sense. Some of the weirder (to me) objects that lived in my mother's china press—a baby bootie encrusted in a sandy glaze, for instance—have their origins in an old and powerful impulse to preserve fleeting time.

Licence mentioned a category of thing related to souvenirs: fairings, so called because they were often carted home as prizes from fairs. Now collectibles, these small china scenes and figurines look to a 21st-century eye like just the thing to clog a mantelpiece or side table. I spent some time browsing eBay's

UK site in search of fairings, and was rewarded with a parade of miniature lads and lasses, husbands and wives, sellers of fruits and vegetables, and assorted animals captured in painted porcelain. To judge by their share of the stock for sale on eBay, the German firm of Conta and Boehme must have cornered the 19th-century market for fairings. For £11.95 (less than $20), a Victorian match striker shaped like a cherub-cheeked lad decked out in a top hat and a nightshirt can grace your mantelpiece, as the seller assures you it did every Victorian fireplace—"how would we light our candles otherwise."

Most of the fairings for sale on eBay serve up commentaries on life romantic and domestic. "Twelve months after marriage" depicts a couple in bed holding a baby. "Kiss me quick" features a lad and lass in the early glow of courtship, going in for a smooch. One feels for the husband in "Home at one o'clock in the morning," his plans to sleep off the night's festivities about to be rudely interrupted by his wife. Happier, and saucier, are the couple in nightcaps and decorous nightwear, sitting up in bed as they contemplate the question "Shall we sleep first or love?"

You might or might not find fairings charming—to me they feel more creepy than delightful—but they are the kind of Victorian decorative object that confirm my worst impressions of the age. Surely Victorians sometimes felt the same way about these tchotchkes and wanted to toss them all in the rubbish bin.

Tom Licence's excavations reveal occasional evidence of a household purge. "Every so often the Victorians enjoyed having a clear-out," he told me. That was often the case when someone died or new owners took possession of a house. Licence particularly associates the phenomenon with upper-middle-class households, which had the means to accumulate and later to discard china and tchotchkes.

In 1895, the Rev. John Francis Kendall, his wife, and their four children moved into the rectory in Hempstead, a village in Norfolk, England. "Arriving at the rectory and heading up the drive, the Kendalls would have been greeted by a brick-built privy with a commodious cesspit," Licence writes in his book. Before long, the new occupants of the rectory decided to stop using the privy, probably because of the availability of indoor plumbing and the smell and possible health risks (typhoid was a big concern) created by the cesspit. So it became a tip, a dumping ground not for human waste but for household discards.

"When the new rector took over in 1885, his family evidently cleared out a load of stuff," Licence told me. "It's what we'd call a clear-out assemblage." Some purges were happier than others, then as now. One imagines the Kendalls and their young family (not to mention servants) bustling around the new house, tossing things to clear space for their own belongings as they settled in. Among the items Licence excavated from the former privy were at least eight serving plates with a blue transfer-printed pattern and dating to the early decades of the 19th century. "Made between 1809 and 1834 by Thomas and Benjamin Godwin of Burslem, they were at least sixty years old when discarded and may have been cleared out of a cupboard either as the remnant of an old dinner service or as tatty pieces no longer suitable for table," Licence writes. "Perhaps they were lurking in a corner, left by the previous rector."

About a decade and a half after the Kendall family moved into their Norfolk rectory, a widow named Mary Everett died at the age of sixty-seven in Falkenham, some 65 miles away in Suffolk on the English coast. Everett left behind two thirtysomething daughters, Kate and Emma Everett. It fell to them, lucky things, to clear out the family house before the property was sold. Licence and a colleague excavated a pond that served as the last resting place of many of Mary Everett's everyday belongings. There's no record of how Kate and Emma Everett felt about having to go through their mother's things, but it's clear from the assemblage Licence excavated that the daughters did a mass purge. "They seemed to have cleared out all her stuff, from medicine bottles to knick-knacks," even a small Chinese vase, he told me.

As an only child, I envied Kate and Emma having each other to lean on as they went through their mother's things. Then again, people have different ideas about what counts as clutter, and at least I had no one to argue with me over the discard decisions I made. Did the Everett sisters ever argue over what was trash and what was treasure? That's a question not so easily answered by archaeology.

One era's clutter becomes another's archaeological record. Found items from the Falkenham pond cleanout constitute a catalog of pantry and medicine-cabinet essentials: "vessels with corks and/or contents still inside," including piccalilli, "a jar for cream or cosmetics, sold by Boots Cash Chemists, discarded with lid and contents," and "a favorite remedy for chest complaints, Congreve's Balsamic elixir," touted as good for coughs, whooping cough, and asthma.

That last item sounds like the Vicks VapoRub of its time, the kind of item that tends to linger in the back of a cabinet for years, only to be flung into the garbage by whoever has to do the final clear-out. I pitched three or four bottles of rubbing alcohol and Epsom salts and a hotel's worth of travel-sized shampoos and conditioners when I emptied out my mother's linen closet. The mention of another bottle from the pond, this one for "Day, Son and Hewitt's gaseous fluid, for curing colic in horses and scour in sheep," put me in mind of the basket in my mother's house of flea shampoos and anti-itch treatments acquired for a parade of cats and dogs over many years and never discarded, even after the animals had died and been reduced to ashes in small wooden boxes with brass labels.

Items that Victorian households no longer wanted didn't all get dumped in privies and ponds—far from it. There wouldn't have been enough ponds in all of Britain.

Unlike me, Kate and Emma Everett couldn't pile their mother's discards in the car and cart them off to Goodwill. Luckily for households that needed to get rid of excess stuff, especially in urban centers, Goodwill came to them. Victorian Britain sustained a network of "street-finders," scavengers and peddlers who collected, traded, and resold everything from rags and bones to outworn clothes and furniture to bottles and scrap metal and coal ash.

Nobody knew or recorded this second-hand economy better than Henry Mayhew, a journalist known best for his series of dispatches for the *Morning Chronicle* newspaper in 1861-62. In those reports, gathered in book form as *London Labour and the London Poor*, Mayhew captured the astonishing range of reused and repurposed resources his fellow Londoners depended on. The system also helped process the prodigious amount of waste produced by so many people living in tight urban quarters.

The reuse-everything mindset sprang out of necessity rather than some proto eco-friendly or sustainability mindset. "In London, where many, in order to live, struggle to extract a meal from the possession of an article which seems utterly worthless, nothing must be wasted," Mayhew writes in a long section called "Of the Street-Sellers of Second-Hand Articles":

> Many a thing which in a country town is kicked by the penniless out of their path even, or examined and left as meet only for the scavenger's cart, will in London be

snatched up as a prize; it is money's worth. A crushed and torn bonnet, for instance, or, better still, an old hat, napless, shapeless, crownless, and brimless, will be picked up in the street, and carefully placed in a bag with similar things by one class of street-folk—the STREET-FINDERS. And to tempt the well-to-do to sell their second-hand goods, the street-trader offers the barter of shapely china or shining glass vessels; or blooming fuchsias or fragrant geraniums for "the rubbish," or else, in the spirit of the hero of the fairy tale, he exchanges, new lamps for old.

Imagine what contemporary city life would be like if people regularly came down your street and offered to swap for or buy up your castoffs, sparing you the trouble of a drive to the dump—and giving you a bit of extra money in the bargain. (Not to mention some blooming fuchsias or fragrant geraniums.) That's a far more satisfying and human-scale vision of sustainable living than I get when the big city truck blasts down my alley once a week to empty the recycling bins into its maw—an uncertain and possibly doomed attempt to reclaim still-useful resources that residents no longer need or want.

It would be dangerous to romanticize the Victorian era as a model for sustainability. Many of the environmental problems that confront today's world have their roots in the industrial age and its insatiable appetite for energy and raw materials, no matter the ecological and social costs of satisfying that hunger.

Even so, what would a workable, modern version of Victorian London's secondhand economy look like in today's urban centers and post-industrial cities? I see glimmers of an answer in adaptations and behavioral shifts creeping into consumer life, like buy-local movements and city laws that encourage shoppers to bring reusable bags to the grocery store. Such programs represent real progress toward sustainability, but they're patchwork solutions that tend to be easiest for relatively affluent urban dwellers to embrace. Imagine what might be possible if people started treating their extra stuff—all the effluvium of modern consumer life—as a resource rather than a nuisance to be organized, stressed about, dumped at a donation center that might or might not want it, or dispatched to the landfill.

In Henry Mayhew's day, a Londoner in search of second-hand items did not have to wait for a street-seller to come down the lane with a cart. He or she could visit one of the city's resale establishments—what we'd probably call a thrift store today, although the term doesn't do justice to the range of what Victorian "rag and bone" shops offered.

To set the scene of these secondhand emporia, Mayhew— no mean observer—turned to another keen-eyed witness of urban life: Charles Dickens. Here's Mayhew quoting Dickens, "one of the most minute and truthful of observers," on the "incongruous mass" of items for sale in these establishments:

> The reader must often have perceived in some by-street, in a poor neighborhood, a small dirty shop, exposing for sale the most extraordinary and confused jumble of old, worn-out, wretched articles, that can well be imagined. Our wonder at their having ever been bought, is only to be equalled by our astonishment at the idea of their ever being sold again. On a board, at the side of the door, are placed about twenty books—all odd volumes; and as many wine-glasses—all different patterns; several locks, an old earthenware pot full of rusty keys; two or three gaudy chimney ornaments—cracked, of course;

the remains of a lustre, without any drops; a round frame like a capital O, which once held a mirror; a flute complete with the exception of the middle joint; a pair of curling-irons and a tinder-box.

Dickens follows this up with a typically giddy catalog of furniture, including chairs "with spinal complaints and wasted legs" and "an incalculable host of miscellanies of every description, including armor and cabinets, rags and bones, fenders and street-door knockers, fire-irons, wearing-apparel and bedding, a hall-lamp, and a room-door."

Some second-hand shops were known as marine stores because of their original purpose, which was to buy and sell sailors' clothing and other nautical gear. As Dickens' catalog demonstrates, they expanded well beyond that. To compare them to contemporary thrift stores doesn't do justice to their variety.

For students of clutter, Dickens remains the 19th-century author to beat in terms of descriptive power. A favorite of mine is the scene in *A Christmas Carol* in which Ebenezer Scrooge, accompanied by the terrifyingly silent Ghost of Christmas Future, watches in horror as a laundress, a charwoman, and an "undertaker's man" haul bundles of a dead man's clothes and bedding—it's Scrooge's, though he doesn't know it—to sell to a marine-store dealer named Joe. They've scavenged everything of any possible value, from silver spoons to the bed curtains and even the suit the deceased was to be buried in.

Heartless, yes, but also economical. Even in an age of mercantilism and excess, nothing need go to waste.

Dickens really outdid himself on the clutter front with Mr. Krook's iconic "rag and bottle" shop in *Bleak House*, a clearinghouse-turned-graveyard of almost anything that could be turned into a commodity. The explosion in newspapers and magazines and broadsides and other print materials over the course of the 19th century created a hunger for paper, usually made out of rags—hence their prominence in the second-hand trade and in the description of Krook's shop. The proprietor apparently buys just about everything: not just rags and bones but old iron, wastepaper, men's and women's clothing, and much more.

Even leftover cooking grease had a secondhand market in Victorian cities. Here's Mayhew on the differences between Krook's kind of emporium and marine stores: "The rag-and-bottle and the marine-store shops are in many instances but different names for the same description of business," he writes. "The chief distinction appears to be this: the marine-store shopkeepers (proper) do not meddle with what is a very principal object of traffic with the rag-and-bottle man, the purchase of dripping, as well as of every kind of refuse in the way of fat or grease."

My personal favorite secondhand shop in Dickens, though, is that run by Mr. Venus, the "articulator of bones," in *Our Mutual Friend*—a book that is itself overstuffed with all manner of wonderful curiosities. Mr. Venus's "little dark greasy shop" is chock full of anatomical surprises. The proprietor, who catalogs them for his villainous guest Mr. Wegg, pronounces his Vs as Ws (so "wise" for "vise"):

Let me show you a light. My working bench. My young man's bench. A Wise. Tools. Bones, various. Skulls, various. Preserved Indian Baby. African ditto. Bottled preparations, various. Everything within reach of your hand, in good preparation. The moldy ones a-top. What's in those hampers over them again, I don't quite remember. Say, human various. Articulated English baby. Dogs. Ducks. Glass eyes, various. Mummied bird. Dried cuticle, various. Dear me! That's the general panoramic view.

Mr. Venus peddles a particularly macabre assortment of clutter, but those with less outlandish items to sell found ready markets for them. In *Victorian Things*, Asa Briggs makes an observation that led me to think Victorians would have found yard sales and Craigslist more familiar than alien. " 'Bring-and-buy sales' were favorite means of disposing both of new and of second-hand things," he writes.

Briggs calls attention to another popular outlet by which Victorians could rehome unwanted items: Sellers could advertise goods "at ten words for a penny in *Exchange and Mart*"—a journal "through which to buy, sell, or exchange anything."

When *Exchange and Mart* said anything, it meant *anything*. Briggs points to an example from an early issue: " 'I have a very handsome curly, liver-colored retriever . . . which I should like to exchange for any good ornament for the drawing room. I am open to offers,'" one early advertiser posted.

"The first category listed in its pages when it began publishing in 1868 was 'bric-a-brac,'" writes Judith Flanders in *Inside the Victorian Home*. "It is hard to imagine how matches were found for the various items described, yet the success of the magazine indicated that they were."

Mathematical instruments, stamps, perambulators, feathers and lace, every sort of tool and animal—Flanders isn't exaggerating about the unexpected variety of items that traded hands. Every item under the sun appears to have found its way into the pages of *Exchange and Mart* sooner or later—very much like Craigslist today. *Exchange and Mart* lasted as a print publication until 2009, when it joined the great digital migration of magazines and newspapers and became online-only.

The internet hasn't yet killed, if it ever will, the lingering Victorian habits of acquisition and display. Behind my house in Washington, DC, there's an old set of garages from the 1920s that have become storage units. I rented one to house the things I salvaged from my mother's house, including that china press that lived for years in her dining room. Where it lived before it came to my mother's house I don't know. It has the been-there-forever air of a family servant who just won't retire or die. The plain, gloomy piece of furniture spent decades as a shrine to stuff. Its lower half held tureens and pieces of serving-ware that waited behind closed doors for special occasions that became more and more infrequent over the decades. On a shelf beside them, a silverware box held a collection of seldom-used cutlery: oyster forks shaped like tiny claws, fish knives with mother-of-pearl handles, butter tongs, the tiniest of spoons for jam and salt.

In public view, the upper shelves housed a small museum of family objects and collectibles, some dating to my great-grandparents' days. Glassware, china figurines, salt cellars to match the tiny spoons down below all jockeyed for space on the dim shelves. Newer arrivals filled in the gaps between the older artifacts like latecomers squeezing into a crowd. If we'd been ancient Romans instead of modern Americans, this cabinet, instead of being a shrine to oyster forks and Wedgwood, might have housed *lares*, our ancestral gods, preserving the spirits of our forebears. Indeed, long before I emptied it out, it had come to feel like a graveyard.

When I was a child, to me the most interesting and perplexing items displayed on the china press were, as I look back, souvenirs not of places but of people. The baby bootie rolled in what looks like sand and then glazed for posterity is the circa-1900 equivalent of a framed infant footprint today, something for nostalgic parents to treasure long after the baby in question grows up and moves on to bigger things. It might have been my mother's or my grandmother's. I don't know if I ever knew. The family memories that made it important enough to earn a place on the public shelves have sunk in the generational stream.

Clutter derives partly from such emotional slippage. Objects outlast the memory of their significance and the people who carried that memory. The bootie at least retains some essence that's familiar: *This belonged to a child who mattered to someone.* Even if I don't know the name of that child and his or her exact relationship to me, I understand the desire to capture a new parent's joy and pride in tangible form.

When I cleaned out the china press, I consigned much of its contents to Goodwill. I spared the vase because I've known it all my life, and because it contains the last of the potpourri that my mother used to love, but I don't remember who brought it into the family in the first place, or why.

One more generation and even the fitfully flickering nostalgia these objects still inspire will be lost for good. Maybe their status as curiosities will save them from the disinterest of my children's generation. Or maybe it won't. The consumer tide keeps rolling in, bringing new things to dispose of, as it has done since long before that china press was made.

CHAPTER 3

Shop and Drop: From Mail-Order Catalogs to Amazon Prime

While Victorian England's street sellers stoked the second trade, Britain's former American colonies cultivated a growing desire for consumer goods and the means to satisfy it. Peddlers travelled the country to bring goods to small towns and isolated homesteads far from urban commercial centers.

But it was a Midwestern city—Chicago—that served as the incubator for an idea that cut out the traveling middleman and put goods in the hands of consumers all over the country. Mail-order catalogs held far more items than even the best-stocked peddler's pack or cart ever could. They could reach anywhere the new railroads and the expanding US postal service did. In the late 19th century, they became a powerful tool to create and satisfy nascent consumer demand beyond the precincts of major metropolitan areas.

Much credit (or blame, depending on how you feel about catalogs) goes to a Chicago-based traveling salesman, Aaron Montgomery Ward. He spotted an opportunity as he visited the rural communities where many of his customers lived: They wanted a greater variety of goods, and at lower prices, than they could get at local stores. So in 1872, Ward created the nation's first mail-order catalog. It was all of one page long but, Jeff Bezos-like, he lost no time expanding his original business model. The *Encyclopedia of Chicago* recaps some of the high points: In 1875, Ward added a "satisfaction guaranteed or your money back" pledge, creating consumer expectations that live on in the Amazon Prime era. The Montgomery Ward catalog enjoyed the kind of exponential growth today's startups dream of. What began as a single-page list of goods swelled to 32 pages by 1876, and by the end of the century it filled nearly 1,000 pages, which puts many a Victorian blockbuster novel to shame.

We have another Midwesterner, a former railway clerk and watch-seller named Richard W. Sears, to thank for the most famous catalog of them all, the Sears & Roebuck "Big Book." Born in Minnesota in 1863, Sears set up shop in Minneapolis as a purveyor of mail-order watches. In 1888, Sears began to advertise his watches via printed mailers. In 1893, he moved the business to Chicago and, in partnership with Alvah C. Roebuck, expanded it into Sears & Roebuck. The following year, the Big Book was born.

The 1894 catalog included "sewing machines, sporting goods, musical instruments, saddles, firearms, buggies, bicycles, baby carriages, and men's and children's clothing"—a range that calls to mind the anything-and-everything range of products available online through Amazon 120 years later. In 1897, the Big Book incorporated full-color spreads, and by 1903, according to the Sears corporate archive, it had gone full color and included everything from barber's chairs to basketballs, not to mention hundreds of other goods and sundries.

This was huge, in every sense. The *Encyclopedia of Chicago* describes the impact of the mail-order flood on the national economy:

> By 1919, Americans were buying over $500 million worth of goods a year from mail-order companies (roughly half of this business went to Wards and Sears alone) . . . Particularly in rural areas, which were still home to half of the American population as late as 1920, the catalogs served not only as a

marketing tool, but also as school readers, almanacs, symbols of abundance and progress, and objects of fantasy and desire.

As an example of entrepreneurial vision enabled by changing technologies, the mail-order catalog counts as a resounding success. And while it put useful and necessary items within the literal reach of households all over the country, it also helped create a never-ending cycle of consumption and desire that ensnared my mother, and many others, decades later.

"Objects of fantasy and desire" sums up my mother's attitude toward the hundreds of catalogs that found their way to her house each year. I do not remember ever seeing a Sears catalog in the house during my childhood, but every day's mail brought another batch: L.L. Bean, calculated to appeal to her Yankee love of practical clothing; White Flower Farm, a gardener's fantasy showcase of tulip bulbs and everything else plantable; the Vermont Country Store, the source of Mom's favorite cranberry-red sheepskin slippers; and Harry & David and Garnet Hill and Lands' End and on through forests' worth of other offerings.

Mom would call me up to tell me she'd seen a few things she thought the kids would like in L.L. Bean's or Oriental Trading Company's latest offerings, or that the King Arthur Flour company had mini-donut pans and wouldn't that be fun to try? (She bought us one of the pans and one of the mixes and yes, making mini-donuts is fun, although the pan gets used maybe once every two years and otherwise just takes up storage space.)

It came as no surprise to me that junk mail, much of it in the form of catalogs, made up a not-insignificant portion of the paper clutter I cleaned out of my mother's house. Get on one mailing list and you wind up on dozens. The Ward and Sears-inspired idea of a catalog as an event persisted long after the catalogs themselves moved online. My mother rarely recycled any of her favorite catalogs until or unless she made time to sit down and browse through them.

What's changed since the Big Book's heyday is how much time consumers have to give to them, along with how many other ways we have to get the things we need and want. There is not enough time in the world for anyone to browse through all the catalogs that still come in the mail, not to mention all the marketing emails that follow purchases.

And yet, amid the instability of modern American life, catalogs can always be relied on to keep coming. Mailing lists spawn more mailing lists, and getting off them requires almost superhuman effort. My mother's junk mail now comes to me. I've signed up for all the opt-out services I know of, and every week I get on the phone with 800-number operators and ask, sometimes politely, sometimes sternly, to be removed from mailing lists, but the mailings just keep coming. In a commercial system where getting added to direct-mail list is the default, the consumer has to work hard, too hard, to opt out. It's easier to let it all pile up.

You might think that the digital era would have killed off the print catalog. Not so. The volume of marketing mail has dropped a bit over the past few years—from 80 billion pieces delivered in 2015 to 75.7 billion in 2019, according to the US Postal Service—but that's still a heck of a lot of catalogs, fliers, and other marketing materials stuffed through mail slots and into mailboxes. In 2017, the *Los Angeles Times* reported that print catalogs were enjoying a renaissance even as their numbers shrank. "Consumers are getting fewer catalogs in the mail these days, 9.8 billion in 2016 compared to the 2007 peak at 19.6 billion," the paper's Ronald D. White reported, "but they're paying more attention to them than ever." A representative for the Data & Marketing Association told White that in 2016, consumers' response to catalogs was up 23 percent from a year earlier. ("Response" here means catalog-inspired purchases.)

If that uptick seems odd, given the digital direction the world continues to take, consider the comfort factor of a tangible object like a print catalog, coupled with the consumer fantasies it lays out on those glossy pages. For my mother, catalogs represented a good life to aspire to and dream about, filled with needfuls and grace notes, with cozy sheepskin slippers from the Vermont Country Store and practical presents for the grandkids from Lands' End.

Clutter derives not only from delayed decisions but from such material cravings, which catalogs exist to satisfy and feed. "A ritualistic form of relaxation" is how Elizabeth Chin describes her addiction to browsing through them. In her book *My Life With Things: The Consumer Diaries*, the anthropologist and media-design professor describes how she likes to settle in with these glossy daydreams: "I hardly ever buy anything at all but can spend hours (yes, hours) thumbing through a catalog and even filling out the forms, all in a game of pretend purchase and possession."

The enduring attachment to catalogs might seem trivial, but it is a reminder that the wild success of Ward and Sears' experiment at the end of the 19th century helped set the stage for a new American century of consumerism.

Historian Susan Strasser has pioneered the study of the evolution of waste and trash in America. Her 1999 book *Waste and Want: A Social History of Trash* remains a pillar of the field more than two decades after its publication. In an interview, Strasser described to me the decades between the 1880s and the 1920s as a watershed in the history of stuff. "I think it's possible to say that the 1880 world looks completely different from the 1920 world," Strasser told me.

She explained how now-familiar consumer items went

from unheard-of novelties to aspirations over the space of a few decades. "In 1880, nobody had a flashlight or a record player or a car," she said. "In 1920, there's a gazillion consumer goods that not everybody had, but everybody knew about them. It's a complete world change." A few more decades and those aspirations became realities for millions of post–World War II Americans.

Means, desire, and opportunity combined to push consumption to new heights: Industrialization and mass production fueled the cycle of consumption, producing more things for more people more quickly. Ward's and Sears' large-scale mail-order experiment in how to create and satisfy consumer demand wouldn't have been possible without a revolution in how goods were manufactured in industrial centers in the Midwest and elsewhere. As with catalogs, the transcontinental network of railroads and the expansion of the postal system made it possible to get those goods into the hands of buyers all over the country.

This expansion of delivery systems delivered substantial social benefits for some groups. Strasser noted how many Americans had been cut off from consumer markets by racism or location. For instance, "black people who lived in the South who wouldn't go to a store could order stuff," she told me. People who lived in rural areas could, too.

Mail-order catalogs enabled those consumers to get products they needed and wanted. That was just the beginning. By 1920 radio had arrived, making it possible for companies to target customers not just via mail, as Sears and Ward had done, but over the airwaves. Illustrated magazines carried ads in living color for products that didn't exist a few decades earlier.

The advent of consumer credit made it possible for households to acquire items they couldn't pay for all at once. As journalist Stephen Smith pointed out in an NPR feature on "The American Dream and Consumer Credit," Americans were already familiar with installment plans, which date back to the Civil War. And there was a lot of new stuff to buy. As Smith noted: "By the early 20th century, increasingly efficient American factories churned our more and cheaper products, like washing machines, refrigerators, phonographs and radios. Most of them could be bought on installment."

My grandparents and great-grandparents grew up in that 1880-1920 crucible of consumerism. Spurred on by mass-market producers and advertising-rich media, they responded by developing a consumer identity that my mother took to the next level. Born in 1938, she entered a world going to war. That conflict reached its formal end on September 2, 1945, days before her seventh birthday. The end of World War II freed up money and materials that fed a growing middle-class appetite in the United States for the trappings of the good life in peacetime: new cars, new houses in new suburbs, new appliances and furnishings to put in those houses. By the time she was a teenager, the postwar era of prosperity was in full swing. Americans got the message that, after so many years of Depression and war, spending money on consumer goods was neither selfish nor frivolous but downright patriotic.

This created a second wave of consumer desire, described by journalist Jason Sanborn in "America's Clutter Problem," a 2015 essay published in *Time* magazine:

> Television blinked into American homes, and advertisers and marketers discovered subtle and subconscious ways of sweet-talking consumers. The idea of planned obsolescence became popular after General Motors discovered that if it developed a new automobile model each year, it could trigger people into upgrading when they otherwise wouldn't. Economists, meanwhile, realized that consumption was vital for the expanding nation."

Patriotism, then, meant buying stuff. "Ensuring a prosperous peacetime would require making new kinds of products and selling them to different kinds of markets," Historian Lizabeth Cohen wrote in the *Journal of Consumer Research* in 2004. "A wide range of economic interests and players all came to endorse the centrality of mass consumption to a successful reconversion from war to peace."

Americans trained to scrimp and save and buy war bonds had to be coaxed back into consumerism. The trick was to appeal to their sense of the greater welfare.

This observation of Cohen's stands out for me because it gets at the fervor with which my mother shopped in the postwar years: "Wherever one looked in the aftermath of war, one found a vision of postwar America where the general good was best served not by frugality or even moderation, but by individuals pursuing personal wants in a flourishing mass consumption marketplace," she writes. "Private consumption and public benefit, it was widely argued, went hand in hand."

In 1955, the year my mother turned seventeen, a marketing consultant and economist named Victor Lebow published an article in the *Journal of Retailing* called "Price Competition in 1955." In spite of that unsexy title, Lebow's article has had a remarkable afterlife in conversations about the history of consumerism in the United States, largely because of this often-quoted description of how the US economy's success depends on linking what we buy to who we are:

> Our enormously productive economy demands that we make consumption our way of life, that we convert the buying and use of goods into rituals, that we seek our spiritual satisfactions, our ego satisfactions, in consumption. The measure of social status, of social acceptance, of prestige, is now to be found in our consumptive patterns.

Lebow often gets cast as the theorist of postwar American hyperconsumption in critical analyses of the phenomenon. In "The Story of Stuff," her influential and powerful 2007 short movie about the human and environmental costs of the "materials economy"—the cycle of extraction, production, distribution, consumption, and disposal—activist Annie Leonard says that Lebow "articulated the solution that has become the norm for the whole system."

When I read Lebow's article in its entirety, though, and took a closer look at that infamous quote, I read is as more diagnostic than prescriptive. A whiff of disapproval or dismay hangs around it. Either way, Lebow was on to something in his assessment.

The conflating of public values and private desires, including the desire for profit, got messier as the 20th century wore on. During this period, new American houses began to expand, which meant more space to fill. "The average number of square feet per person in the median new home nearly doubled from the 1970s to the 2010s," according to a 2019 *Atlantic* article by Joe Pinsker, in which he examines why homes in the United States tend to be larger than those almost everywhere else in the world. That trend fuels the clutter problem too. Bigger houses go hand in hand with a culture that has long valued having more stuff. The bigger the house, the more space there is to fill with things.

By the early 2000s, the social and familial costs of American hyper consumption were making themselves felt in the nation's homes and garages. In *Life at Home in the Twenty-First Century: 32 Families Open Their Doors*, a team of anthropologists documented the astonishing amount of stuff they found during an ethnographic study of Angeleno families' living spaces from 2001-05. "Never before has any society accumulated so many personal possessions," the authors write.

The study focused on dual-income couples with children, and included families drawn from diverse income brackets, neighborhoods, and ethnicities. In the first "household assemblage" the researchers assessed, they found 2,260 "visible possessions" in two bedrooms and the living room alone—in a relatively small house 980 square feet in size. Such density of possessions turned up again and again in the study. "Small wonder that quite a few of the sampled L.A. houses, which average 1,750 square feet of living space, feel overstuffed and cluttered," the researchers noted.

The inhabitants of those overstuffed houses felt it too, as they revealed in "self-narrated tours" of their living quarters. The takeaway, which will feel familiar to anyone confronting an overstuffed house: "Many find their accumulated possessions exhausting to contemplate, organize, and clean."

I am not an ethnographer, but from everything I have seen, a similar sense of overwhelm persists in American households nearly two decades later. The forces that combine to create it have, if anything, ramped up since those Angelenos opened their homes in the early years of the century. To love someone is to provide for that person with food, shelter, clothing—all tangible forms of care. As the capitalist gears ground away in the second half of the 20th century, the rising emphasis on consumption exploited these better instincts.

Elizabeth Chin argues in *My Life With Things* that consumers are trained from early days to become "commodity fetishists" in a Marxist sense: Beginning with the first lovey they receive babies, children are taught to look to objects as sources of emotional stability. "The ritual gift of that first stuffed toy is also the first step in training individuals to put their trust in things, not people," Chin writes. "It's really quite a strange practice."

Is it? These plush nonhuman friends inhabit a child's imaginative universe in ways that do not involve commerce (after the initial purchase or gift). Penelope the Platypus and Buffles the Bear, my kids' favorite stuffed toys, have had many adventures and inspired some of our family's enduring jokes and songs. I still have my childhood owl, Ostrobogalus, on top of my wardrobe, though after five decades he looks shabbier than an owl ought to.

Chin's right, though, that mainstream, middle-class US culture encourages children from their earliest days to invest emotions in *things*. This starts even before a baby arrives, as parents-to-be accumulate clothes and gear for the impending bundle of joy. Depending on their means, parents spend large amounts of time and money to decorate and furnish nursery spaces for their offspring, conflating love and stuff.

While cash-flush Manhattanites don't have much in common with most of us—the rich really are different from you and me—what they're willing to spend on nursery furnishings says something about the upper-end aspirations pushed on American families. One interior designer based in Murray Hill revealed to the *New York Post* in 2019 that her clients spend $10,000 to $100,000—you read that right—on nursery decor. Another designer in the tri-state area reported that her clients spend between $8,000 and $10,000 to set up nurseries. "The honest truth, I think it's really for social media," she told the *Post* reporter.

While these luxury baby rooms are not necessarily hotbeds of clutter—if you can afford to drop $10K on a nursery, you can probably pay people to keep it neat and clean—the desire to equip our children with the latest things extends far down the socioeconomic spectrum. Over my lifetime, the variety of toys and products marketed to children and their parents has exploded. That lays the groundwork for the clutter problem that besets and exhausts many contemporary US families.

"Children in the US make up 3.1% of the world's kid population, but US families buy more than 40% of the toys purchased globally," Sanborn writes in his *Time* essay.

The playroom clutter I spent many of my early parenting years dealing with has its roots in the postwar era of plastics and prosperity. Mr. Potato Head first appeared in 1952. LEGO came up with its iconic bricks in 1958. Sixty years later, in 2018, it sold about 70 billion "elements." (Via email, a helpful corporate PR person told me that an element equals "any piece produced by LEGO," not just bricks but other components like tires; it takes 9 or 10 elements to create one minifigure.) In 2018, LEGO's flagship factory in Billund, Denmark, produced about 100 million elements a day.

I can't count just how many "elements" wound up scattered through our family playroom during the heyday of my son's LEGO obsession a few years ago. The most ambitious set he built, the Millennium Falcon model, contains 1,329 pieces. Add to that the dozens of sets given to him by generous relatives and friends over the years and we're probably talking 10,000 plastic bits, maybe more. And that's just one family's stash.

My son loved those LEGOs, and the hours he spent building and creating with them were not wasted. Would he have been happy with one shoebox full of them? Very likely. But the thrill of the new, focused on branded sets like the Millennium Falcon and reinforced by friends' acquisitions and the LEGO magazine that arrived monthly in the mail, made sure his collection kept expanding until it defeated all attempts to keep it under control. I lost too many hours attempting to organize and contain the clutter via a system of plastic shoeboxes labeled "Minifigures," "Small bricks," and so forth.

The playrooms of the near future may have fewer LEGO booby-traps. In the fall of 2019, The company announced a pilot recycling program in the United States. Customers can ship old LEGOs back to the company, which will clean and redistribute them via Teach for America and some Boys & Girls Clubs. LEGO's vice president of environmental responsibility—all large companies should have one—said the move came in response to customer demand. Saving the planet and freeing ourselves from clutter go hand in hand.

The 1960s, the decade of my birth, ushered in another consumer revolution in the United States: the rise of the big-box store, packed with discounted items to snap up and cart off to increasingly full American homes. As a high schooler and then college student in the 1980s, I remember how shopping centers anchored by big-box chains metastasized along the major arterials connecting the suburbs that ring my hometown of Washington, DC. The same phenomenon was taking place all over the country in the latter years of the 20th century. No wonder my mother often seemed most at home, most herself, in the consumer spaces of postwar America. In that, too, she fell victim to another turn in American life described by Lizabeth Cohen in *A Consumers' Republic*: the rise of the shopping center, "where the center of community life was a site devoted to mass consumption."

A 2015 research roundup from Harvard's Shorenstein Center on Media, Politics, and Public Policy called 1962 "year zero" in the history of big-box stores in the United States. The first Walmart, Target, and Kmart stores opened that year. These stores and others like them, focused on moving more products at cheaper prices, encouraged consumers like my mother to buy more—often more than they needed. The desire to find a bargain has long been part of the American consumer's economic DNA, but the marketing innovations of the last half-century have turned that desire into a handicap that drains wallets and fills up living spaces.

If you can buy ten boxes of paperclips for the cost of one, it's easy to think first of the bargain you're getting. Only later, when you're stuffing all those boxes into desk drawers, do you realize you don't need or have room for them.

I have a voice memo I recorded on my phone one summer afternoon as I sat in my mother's desk chair and sifted through the contents of her home office, trying to figure out what to do with it all. The room itself was barely big enough for one tall filing cabinet, an L-shaped desk, and a set of wire shelves. But that space contained multitudes, as captured by my despair-inflected recording:

Hundreds of pens and pencils, stored in six different containers on the desk and stuffed in drawers. Dozens of Sharpies. Old snapshots of my kids. Post-It notes, every size and description. Tiny screwdrivers. An ancient comb. More tiny screwdrivers. Old pills. Shopper loyalty cards from various stores. Weird random crap I could not identify. A big marble. A spool of blue thread. Bobby pins, safety pins. More weird random crap. Key rings, business cards from people she had not done business with in years. A token for the New York City Metro. Some sort of gold coin. A mini Allen wrench device. S hooks. Cartridges for fountain pens. Tiny little locks for luggage. Rabies tags for pets long dead, with the ashes of the pets themselves in boxes on the shelves nearby. Screws, safety pins, paper clips, more paper clips, still more paper clips. Lapel buttons. A crucifix. (That was unexpected.) At least 50 sheets of return-address labels, sent by every charity she supported and many she did not. Stationery with her business logo. Boxes of file folders. Pencil erasers. Bottle openers.

Smooth pebbles. A nail file. Rubber bands. More lapel pins. More luggage locks. A drawer's worth of old calculators and picture hangers and— Oh, good lord, I have no idea what's even in here.

It was unexpectedly soothing to go through all the pens and test them, one by one, to see if they had run dry. Those that worked I boxed up and drove to the animal shelter, along with all the Sharpies and the Post-Its and the file folders and the paper clips. It felt good to release all these things from the limbo in which they had lingered for so long and put them back into circulation, where they might become useful again. To declutter does not always mean to discard; it can be a way to reclaim an object's original purpose.

Whatever my mother's motivations—whether she suffered from chronic disorganization or incipient dementia or a combination of factors that primed her to acquire and hold on to more stuff than she could ever use—she fell victim to a system that makes it too easy to buy more than we need. Cheaper by the dozen: Buy in bulk and save money, the theory goes. Maybe so, but the costs go beyond money. Does one person need to stockpile thousands of paper clips? How many paper clips, rubber bands, or staples does a small business go through every day, week, or month? I have a box of staples that has lasted me for years, even though as a writer and editor I find lots of reasons to staple documents.

It's tempting to think that if you need a couple of pens, it would be smarter to buy a box of ten or twenty or fifty, just in case, even if you don't have to buy for a company with multiple employees who will raid the office-supply closet. As I wrote this section, I swung by the Staples website to check out the deals on writing implements. I discovered I could buy 60-count box of ballpoint pens for the low price of $6.49, with in-store pickup guaranteed in an hour. I could have them delivered to my doorstep the next day if I didn't feel like driving out to the store. (I didn't. But I don't need sixty pens either.)

Maybe it's a salutary thing, from the perspective of overconsumption and clutter, that the big-box, buy-more stores that flourished in the mid- to late 20th century—my mother's prime consumer years—have hit hard times in the second decade of the 21st. Many of the malls that used to be meccas for teens and their parents have aged badly. Some of the big chains that anchored them have closed or reduced their bricks-and-mortar footprints. The term "retail apocalypse" has sprung up to describe this widespread phenomenon of familiar chains shuttering their doors.

It turns out that habits of overconsumption, once established, don't deteriorate like 1980s mall architecture. The buy-more bargain mentality the big retail chains helped create has just migrated online. Even the Great Recession didn't kill it. As the *Washington Post* reported in April 2019 in a story on what's driving the retail apocalypse, the average US household spent $5,200 online in 2018, an increase of nearly 50 percent from five years before.

Recent figures from the US Department of Commerce call attention to our shifting shopping habits. The trade journal *Internet Retailer,* reporting on the department's data in early 2019, concluded that ecommerce represented more than 14 percent of total retail sales in 2018, a rise from 11.8 percent in 2016.

If that sounds relatively minor, consider *Internet Retailer*'s observation that ecommerce sales counted for more than half of all retail sales growth. In other words, what shoppers increasingly don't buy at Target or other big-box stores, they now get with a few clicks online.

Online, products seek out potential buyers as well as the other way around. Thanks to algorithms that track keyword searches and browsing histories, targeted ads pop up as internet users travel from website to website and platform to platform—whether or not those users even went online in order to make a purchase. In December 2019, media-studies professor and author Siva Vaidyanathan pointed out in a *Slate* article that this net of targeted, data-driven advertising has been weaving itself around consumers for almost twenty years, since Google figured out how to peg simple ads to keyword searches.

Unless you have good ad blockers in place, even a brief browse for shoes or swimsuits or almost any other consumer item will generate ads for those items when you click on over to Facebook or your favorite news site. Sometimes the ads create inadvertent comedy, or draw on flawed assumptions and stereotypes—algorithms reflect the biases of their designers—but the net effect is to make buying stuff as hard to resist as possible.

To take a prime example (pun intended), Amazon's one-click shopping makes it dangerously easy to satisfy the desire for more stuff. My family's order history reflects the stunning variety of goods the company makes it oh-so-easy to purchase. Among the dozens (make that hundreds) of items we have ordered in the past year: socks, sunscreen, adult diapers, anime wigs, moisture-wicking tee shirts, computer components, a dog-themed draft stopper, calming treats for a nervous cat, a clip-on light to illuminate an electronic keyboard, and a copy of the Yukio Mishima novel *The Sailor Who Fell from Grace with the Sea*. And that was all before the COVID-19 pandemic, which triggered even more online purchases.

In a digital-era continuation of the grand tradition that Montgomery Ward and Sears helped establish with mail-order catalogs, Amazon has been building this buy-more model, and training consumers' expectations accordingly, for the last quarter-century. Bezos and his then-wife, Mackenzie, founded the company as an online bookseller in 1994, using a garage as HQ. Books were just the beginning. In 2005, Amazon introduced Amazon Prime. The ultimate goal, as journalist Brad Stone describes in his book of the same name, was to create "the everything store." Whatever you think of Amazon's labor and business practices, however useful and economical your Prime membership seems or is (the savings! the streaming! the Whole Foods discounts!), pause to consider that the "everything store" wants you to buy—well, everything.

Amazon Prime members—there were more than 150 million globally as of January 2020, according to Amazon's earnings release for the fourth quarter of 2019—have become spoiled by how fast purchases arrive. Buy it today, enjoy it tomorrow—without the hassle of having to get to a bricks-and-mortar store. Multiply my middle-class family's purchases by millions, and the result is a flood of goods surging from warehouses onto planes and trucks, into the hands of delivery people (often subcontracted to Amazon by the US Postal Service) and into America's living spaces. Jeff Bezos told shareholders that in 2017, Amazon shipped more than 5 billion items through its Prime service.

Five BILLION items. Even if many of our online orders serve useful and necessary functions in our lives (see socks and sunscreen, above), many do not. Many get used only a few times before the novelty wears off and they get tossed in a drawer or closet. Meet the clutter of tomorrow.

Often adding to that clutter is the packaging it came in. Amazon's expedited delivery model creates "a massive hangover of packaging waste," as a 2019 *Washington Post* article on Amazon's switch to lightweight plastic mailers put it. While lightweight mailers take up less room and cost less to ship, they're also harder to recycle, which increases the risk of eco-clutter. "As the platform behind half of all e-commerce transactions in 2018, according to eMarketer, Amazon is by far the biggest shipper and producer of that waste—and a trendsetter, meaning that their switch to plastic mailers could signal a shift across the industry," the *Post* reported.

Mailers aren't the end of it. Independent journalist Emily Atkin dug into the ecological ramifications of Amazon's expansion into home delivery of groceries from Whole Foods, the upscale grocery chain it now owns. The silver freezer bags it uses for those deliveries, like the mailers it uses for other products, can't be recycled. Even worse, according to Atkin, the bags aren't made from recycled material either, which means they eat up more virgin resources.

Apply that to the other corporations and manufacturing enterprises that produce the goods that occupy homes in the United States (and much of the developed world). Atkin cited a 2009 study by the Environmental Protection Agency on carbon emissions, which found that "the way Americans procure, produce, deliver and dispose of goods and services accounted for *nearly half* of the nation's greenhouse gas emissions."

And yet over and over again the focus falls on individual consumers, who are shamed when they fail to recycle, or when they buy too much and let their stuff overwhelm them. Much of the disgrace rightfully belongs to the corporations that built and perpetuate the system in which consumers find themselves enmeshed. Who will save us from all our stuff?

CHAPTER 4

A Place for Everything:
The Endless War on Disorder

For years, my mother complained about her stuff, even as it piled up around her. Just as the roots of modern clutter stretch back centuries, so does the desire to cut through the disorder and live an orderly life.

There's no shortage of advice-givers who stand ready to help (and who dream of making a mint off other people's messes). Today's organizational gurus have more platforms than ever for peddling advice: how-to books, newsletters, TV and radio appearances, podcasts, online courses, Facebook groups, and more. Like the clutter they offer to help cut through, today's crop of decluttering guides grows out of a long tradition that dates back to humanity's early days.

The idea that order creates harmony, and that it signals a virtuous life, stretches back to the earliest human civilizations, as the anthropologist Mary Douglas explores in her classic 1966 book *Purity and Danger*. Specific definitions and interpretations of dirt and disorder vary from culture to culture, but in Douglas's reading, it's a near-universal human experience to associate disorder with immorality or impurity—with living one's life the wrong way. The shame and stigma attached to hoarding disorder keep that old association alive. In industrial economies that enshrine material goods alongside (sometimes in place of) spiritual practices, clutter signals that someone has failed to live the "right" way.

To understand why clutter causes so much agitation—it's just stuff, right?—I find this observation of Douglas's useful: "If we can abstract pathogenicity and hygiene from our notion of dirt, we are left with the old definition of dirt as matter out of place." (I read "dirt" as a stand-in for clutter.) I can't think of a better definition of clutter than "matter out of place." Douglas writes, "This is a very suggestive approach. It implies two conditions: a set of ordered relations and a contravention of that order. Dirt then is never a unique, isolated event. Where there is dirt there is system." Clutter deranges us, or indicates derangement in the sense of something out of alignment. Disordered mind, disordered life.

———

The spiritual stakes of the capitalist way of life feel very high— punitively so, for people like my mother who, for whatever reasons of their own, can't achieve material balance. They're reduced to their things and shamed for not being able to control the onslaught of stuff consumer society hurls at them.

In a 2019 book, *The Enchantments of Mammon: How Capitalism Became the Religion of Modernity*, the historian Eugene McCarraher sets out to show how capitalism offers us "a parody or perversion of our longing for a sacramental way of being in the world." McCarraher, who writes from an explicitly religious perspective, assembles a formidable gallery of evidence to demonstrate how capitalism's acolytes long have pushed us to substitute goods for a good life.

I have been intrigued by the hunger for spiritual cleansing that has gone hand in hand with the latest minimalist outbreak in the United States and beyond. Today's minimalist gurus turn the quest for fewer things into something close to religion. Live simply, that others may simply live: The ghosts of thrift and order, of right living, persist in such sayings, handed down in my family and many others.

Waste not, want not.
Use it up, wear it out, make it do or do without.
A place for everything and everything in its place.

Even a famous line from the movie *Fight Club* could be a distillation of wisdom from a 19th-century domestic-advice manual: "The things you own end up owning you."

This vexed relationship with stuff, at least in the domestic sphere, has long been associated with women. "A Housekeeper's Symphony," a poem credited to Fanny Waugh Davis and published in *Good Housekeeping* in 1907, catalogs all the tasks and responsibilities—"the thousand small things always at hand," a symphony of chores—that fall to the woman of the house. The poem makes gentle fun of the trial of having to live with a family "always late to meals." Then it circles back to the essential responsibility of keeping order: "To try to keep the odds and ends in place.... To know the place for everything and keep it there."

Many modern women know the feeling. That may change as gender roles and identities become more fluid. Still, if you're an adult female, whether you identify as Millennial or Gen X or Boomer, chances are you grew up trained, explicitly or by example, to expect that sooner or later it would be your job to bring order out of chaos.

In spite of all the gains made in the workplace, women still do a disproportionate amount of housework. We're more likely to clean up at the office, too. "Even in 2019, messy men are given a pass and messy women are unforgiven," as an article in *The New York Times* put it. "Three recently published studies confirm what many women instinctively know: Housework is still considered women's work—especially for women living with men." The story included stats from the US Department of Labor: Women spend an average of 2.3 hours a day on house-related work, while men spend 1.4 hours. The struggle continues.

Traditional oppression, traditional expectations that women would keep the household symphony humming along have created business opportunities as well as burdens. Shut out of many professional spheres, a number of women in the Industrial Era found lucrative ways to establish themselves as experts on matters domestic. Faced with social pressures to keep house well and a burgeoning amount of stuff to furnish houses with, the Victorians turned to a cadre of advice mavens (I'm tempted to call them proto-Kondos) who fed a robust appetite for books on domestic economy. Today's organizational bestsellers owe a debt to the writers of early advice manuals, who showed an increasingly materialistic world how it was done.

Prominent among these domestic trailblazers was Isabella Beeton, a young journalist married to a London book and magazine publisher, Sam Beeton. She worked hard and well at her trade, and died far too young, in 1865, at the age of twenty-eight, from a postpartum infection. But in that relatively short life she gave birth to four children while she pursued full-time work as a journalist and editor.

Mrs. Beeton probably did not coin the phrase "A place for everything and everything in its place," which turns up in various iterations over the centuries, but she's forever associated with the sentiment. Her crowning accomplishment was producing a how-to-keep-house blockbuster whose success rivals (or exceeds) any of the manuals produced by Martha Stewart or Marie Kondo. *Mrs. Beeton's Book of Household Management*, a compendium of recipes and advice on how to maintain an "orderly and well-managed" house, sold more than 60,000 copies in Britain when it was published in 1861. By 1868, it had sold two million copies.

Beeton's advice found a vast and appreciative audience in the middle ranks of society. In a review of a biography of Mrs. Beeton, cultural historian Rotskoff describes the typical reader of the book as "a housewife from the low- to mid-level ranks of the middle class: a woman married to a tradesman, clerk, or professional; living in or near a newly industrialized city; and employing, perhaps, one domestic servant, a 'maid of all work' to help with chores and childcare."

Readers of Beeton's work were not moneyed ladies of leisure. They were modestly middle-class women with households to run on limited budgets—the kind of women who today might turn to a professional organizer or advice book when the domestic scene threatens to overwhelm them. Because the hyperabundance that feeds clutter tracks so closely with the rise of mass production and industrialization, *Mrs. Beeton's Book of Household Management* can also be read as a primer on what today would be called productivity. New systems of production required new systems of order.

Rotskoff writes, "Mrs. Beeton won the hearts and minds of her modestly genteel woman readers with a clear, authoritative voice that guided them through life in a rapidly changing world. In essence, she was a bellwether of the industrialization of the home—a process by which the systems, procedures, and values of the mechanized workplace transformed the nature of domestic labor."

While Mrs. Beeton was teaching Victorian British women how best to cook and keep house, women in the United States could turn to a homegrown duo for similar enlightenment. Not long after the Civil War, Harriet Beecher Stowe (of *Uncle Tom's Cabin* fame) joined forces with her sister Catherine E. Beecher to show American housewives how it was done.

In *The American Woman's Home: Or, Principles of Domestic Science* ("Being a Guide to the Formation and Maintenance of Economical, Healthful, Beautiful, and Christian Homes"), published in 1869, the sisters dispensed facts and wisdom on almost all areas of family and home life. They covered hygiene, nutrition, and exercise; explained how to treat different ailments; shared sound scientific information on the principles of good ventilation and many other practical matters; laid out how to build and decorate a model family home on a budget; and much more.

The book includes a substantial chapter on "Habits of System and Order" that begins with advice on how to organize one's schedule and habits of mind along Christian principles. Then it moves on to time-management advice and organizing tips that with some updated vocabulary would be right at home in the toolkit of today's professional organizers:

> Another mode of systematizing relates to providing proper supplies of conveniences, and proper places in which to keep them. Thus, some ladies keep a large closet, in which are placed the tubs, pails, dippers, soap-dishes, starch, blueing, clothes-lines, clothes-pins, and every other article used in washing; and in the same, or another place, is kept every convenience for ironing....

The chapter winds through the spaces of the house, reinforcing the handy notion of "a place appointed for each article." A place for everything and everything in its place.

The Beecher sisters' manual and Isabella Beeton's blockbuster stand as two of the most famous examples of what was (and still is) a thriving market for domestic-economy books, though marketers wouldn't use the term today. The Schlesinger Library, part of the Radcliffe Institute for Advanced Study at Harvard University, maintains an extensive collection of 19th-century advice manuals. A search for "household management" turns up 433 entries, including various editions of Mrs. Beeton's book, but less-famous alternatives and competitors abound, published in both the UK and the United States.

I pulled together a few favorites, omitting some of the lengthy descriptive subtitles that spell out every subsection and category of domestic life covered in each book:

The complete home: an encyclopedia of domestic life and affairs, by Julia McNair Wright (1879)

First principles of household management and cookery: a textbook for schools and families, by Maria Parloa (1882)

Miss Corson's practical American cookery and household management, by Juliet Corson (c. 1885)

Mrs. Parker's complete housekeeper: a system of household management for all who wish to live well at a moderate cost, by Eliza R. Parker (1888)

The 19th- and early-20th-century popularity of such domestic advice books feels very contemporary. Over the decades, though, the waste-not, want-not ethos behind them got lost in the consumerist race to accumulate.

As historian Susan Strasser explains in *Waste and Want*, much of the early advice aimed at housekeepers focused on how to make the most use of limited resources. "Without trash collectors or much cash for purchases, most nineteenth-century American women had to make do with whatever was at hand instead of solving problems with products," she writes. "Books of advice for farm women and urban housekeepers were full of ideas for using stored materials."

Coal ashes, corncobs, ashes, even tea leaves could be put to good use. (Used tea leaves would "brighten the looks of a carpet, and prevent dust.") What would a 19th-century housewife make of contemporary clutter? The current emphasis on purging and discarding excess items would likely appall a reader of 19th-century advice manuals.

I see glimmers of hope in the recent popularity of the mantra "Reduce, reuse, recycle." Even though it's deployed most often by relatively affluent and eco-conscious consumers, who have the means and time to put it into practice, it points the way to reclaiming the "Waste not, want not" spirit that animated much of the counsel shared by Mrs. Beeton and her contemporary advice mavens. Yesterday's thriftiness has become today's sustainability.

―――――――

For many consumers, thrift has never been a matter of choice or ethics. Not everybody in industrializing Britain and the United States had the means to head to the seashore for sunshine and souvenirs or purchase the trappings of a well-appointed middle-class life. Then as now, personal and household finances constrained individual choices. Many could not afford vacations or souvenirs in the first place; many of the workers who ran the factories that produced the expanding array of consumer goods did not make enough to buy the things they made. Shop workers sold items they couldn't afford to purchase themselves.

Still, there's a rich history of moneyed folk who have opted for simplicity. Even among more well-to-do Victorians, not everyone raced to embrace the plushly furnished lifestyle of the Sambournes. Some, similar to today's minimalist gurus, stood ready to lead consumption-weary acolytes toward a promised land of simpler living. Victorian Britain, obsessed with the domestic sphere, had no shortage of people eager to give advice on how to decorate a home.

So it was with William Morris (1834-1896), a successful broker's son who was born into money but had a complicated relationship with its opulent trappings. Morris grew up in comfort in Walthamstow in then-rural North London. The William Morris Society describes his childhood as idyllic, spent playing with his siblings, reading *The Arabian Nights* and other imagination-stoking tales, and immersing himself in the natural world, an early interest he would later incorporate into designs of intertwining vines and flowers. (You have perhaps seen examples of these designs on wallpaper or ties.)

Morris thought about becoming a priest; instead he turned to art, architecture, and radicalism. The pre-Raphaelite painters Dante Gabriel Rossetti and Edward Burne-Jones were among his close friends and collaborators, as was the architect Philip Webb. Eventually Morris turned to socialism, taking up with Friedrich Engels, among others, but along the way he became a leading light of the Arts & Crafts Movement, with art critic John Ruskin providing some of the philosophical firepower behind it. With an emphasis on craftsmanship over mass production, the movement—also called Mission style on my side of the Atlantic—set itself up as a rebuke to the mass production and cheap consumerism made possible by (and fueling) Victorian manufacturing.

Ruskin held up medieval architecture "as a model for honest craftsmanship and quality materials," wrote Monica Obniski, curator of decorative arts at Atlanta's High Museum, in a 2008 essay on the movement. Ruskin's argument hit home with Morris, "who believed that industrialization alienated labor and created a dehumanizing distance between the designer and manufacturer."

This observation of Obniski's carries particular weight with me: "Morris strove to unite all the arts within the decoration of the home, emphasizing nature and simplicity of form." This serves up a corrective to Victorian excesses of ornamentation and furnishing, an antidote to the consumerist mantra that more is better. For Morris, fewer things, well made, constituted an ideal, not mantelpieces lined with china knickknacks or drawing rooms full of overstuffed and opulent furniture.

Morris found company in spreading the useful-or-beautiful mantra, including British furniture designer and architect Charles Locke Eastlake (1836-1906). The word "clutter" does not turn up in *Hints on Household Taste in Furniture, Upholstery, and Other Details*, Eastlake's influential 1868 home-design guide. But Eastlake has strong words for "knick-knacks ... that heterogeneous assemblage of modern rubbish which, under the head of 'china ornaments' and various other names, finds its way into the drawing-room or boudoir."

Morris took the no-knickknacks principle further. In 1880, he delivered a speech to the Birmingham Society of Arts and School of Design on "The Beauty of Life," about how to encourage the conditions for making art. The big takeaway line from the lecture reads to me like a 19th-century precursor of Marie Kondo's "spark joy" test:

> Believe me, if we want art to begin at home, as it must, we must clear our houses of troublesome superfluities that are forever in our way: conventional comforts that are no real comforts, and do but make work for servants and doctors: if you want a golden rule that will fit everybody, this is it: "HAVE NOTHING IN YOUR HOUSES THAT YOU DO NOT KNOW TO BE USEFUL OR BELIEVE TO BE BEAUTIFUL."

Two years later, Oscar Wilde brought the same idea to

the United States on a speaking tour promoting the Aesthetic Movement. His lecture "The House Beautiful" riffs on (or rips off) Morris: "Have nothing in your houses that is not useful or beautiful; if such a rule were followed out, you would be astonished at the amount of rubbish you would get rid of."

The Washington, DC rowhouse I live in, built in 1922, has built into it a modest, American version of this simplicity-of-form, anti-clutter principle. It's a style known as a daylighter, because the light passes through unobstructed from the front of the house to the back, without a Victorian warren of dark rooms to trap it. Mission-style, it emphasizes rectilinear shapes and natural wood.

It's not fancy, and that too hews to Morris's aesthetic. The people who designed and built my house in 1922 did away with fireplaces, counting on the modern charm of radiators to keep the occupants warm. Maybe, like Frank Lloyd Wright and his long-suffering clients in the American Midwest of the early 20th century, architects and builders decided to minimize the temptation to accrue clutter by doing away with some of its natural gathering spots. Wright (1867-1959) put that principle to work in the United States with his idea of "organic architecture," which touted the idea of simplicity. In the early 1900s, Darwin Martin, a well-heeled businessman in Buffalo, New York, commissioned the Chicago-based architect to design a Prairie-style house for his family.

I toured the Darwin Martin house with my children, then in their bored-tween phase, one summer a few years ago. I mostly remember low ceilings and dim spaces that created the sense of being inside a cave rather than a showplace. The lack of clutter did call attention to the structure and its architectural and ornamental details. The house is famous for its almost 400 pieces of "art glass" designed by Wright and produced by the Chicago-based Linden Glass Company in 1904-5. The most famous of these art-glass installations, a window known as the "Tree of Life," includes more than 750 bits of glass, and it's a wonder. (Even the term "window" was too quotidian for Wright; he preferred "light screen.")

I sensed, in this most highly designed of spaces, the architect's yearning to impose order on the messiness of day-to-day domestic life. The tour didn't answer the question of how the occupants would actually live in such a space, which offered them so little purchase for the trappings of their day to day routines.

Wright dictated that his clients should avoid extraneous furnishings, and he only grudgingly added a mantelpiece—a domestic touch he hated on the theory that it just spawned clutter. There's wisdom in this. In most houses, a mantelpiece *is* a magnet for all manner of items that sit there unused and unnoticed. In theory, then, doing away with the mantelpiece and other clutter hotspots creates the conditions for a home free of unwanted accumulations of stuff.

Hire an architectural visionary to build your house and you sign up for more than living space. A fact sheet created for a renovation of the Darwin Martin House complex a few years ago described Wright's all-in approach:

> Whenever circumstances allowed, Frank Lloyd Wright liked to design the furnishings and fixtures for a house as well as the spaces of the house itself. This was in keeping with his concepts of "organic architecture"— that a house shouldn't be a series of neutral boxes that you would fill up with clutter brought from your previous dwelling. Rather, he saw furniture, carpeting, lighting fixtures, and decorative objects as an integral part of a comprehensive design for living.

Our collective default position, then as now, is that clutter should be kept at bay—that it trips us up on the way to a fulfilled and harmonious life. I tend to agree with that. But on the tour of the Darwin-Martin house I had a passing heretical thought: What if clutter is part of what makes a house a home? My mother's stuff overwhelmed her, and me after her, but it was undeniably hers. As with today's extreme stripped-down minimalist interiors, the Darwin-Martin house looks magnificent but offers little space for residents to be their messy, acquisitive, stuff-strewing selves.

In spite of the long, systemic history behind today's glut of things, American culture continues to be obsessed with clutter on the individual level. Society still puts the burden on individuals to keep things in order.

This collective judginess has created a golden opportunity for a new generation of Mrs. Beetons. For the past five years, one approach to decluttering has dominated the conversation about how to deal with the problem: the KonMari Method™, Japanese organizing guru Marie Kondo's signature approach to "tidying up" homes and lives.

In January 2019, Netflix's *Tidying Up With Marie Kondo* inspired countless clutterbugs to dive into closets and drawers, pull out everything they own, and confront the essential question: "Does it spark joy?" Instagram and Facebook accounts have been swamped with before-and-after photos demonstrating the transformative magic wielded by the chipper Kondo, who in her TV show descends on clients' houses to dispense hugs and gentle encouragement.

Kondo's show brings to life the advice of her bestselling book *The Life-Changing Magic of Tidying Up*, which appeared in English in the fall of 2014. In May 2020, it still occupied the number-one bestseller slot in Amazon's Zen Philosophy and Feng Shui categories. A follow-up, *Spark Joy: An Illustrated Master Class on the Art of Organizing and*

Tidying Up, came out in 2016 and is also a top seller. Her next book, *Joy at Work*, co-authored with Scott Shonenstein, a professor of management at Rice University, extends her methods to messy desks and offices.

I read *The Life-Changing Magic of Tidying Up* as a desperate lark in the murky middle of cleaning out my mother's house, when it seemed the process would never end and I would be battling the chaos forever. At some other point in my life I might have been irritated by Kondo's upbeat style, her relentless optimism, her breezy promise that no mess was too big to conquer if you broke it down pile by pile, in a sequence of five categories: clothes, books, papers, *kimono* (miscellaneous items), and memorabilia or sentimental things.

In the depths of my cleaning-out despair, though, "tidying up" sounded lovely and British, like something Beatrix Potter's Mrs. Tiddlewinks would do, a quiet set of tasks that would bring satisfaction and make everything nice again. The world, full of chaos and mess, needs more orderly, calm, and pleasing spaces. I certainly had more than enough chaos and mess in my life. I was hungry for reassurance that I would not in the end be swallowed up and lost forever in a sea of clutter.

I got through the book in one sitting—on my Kindle app, the better not to clutter my already overfull bookshelves. I did not subject my own house to the full KonMari treatment, but my daughter and I did pile all our clothes on our beds, as Kondo prescribes, and had fun holding everything up and asking ourselves and each other "Does it spark joy?" The domestic changes that ensued, while not dramatic, have persisted, somewhat to my surprise. I now thank my discarded items for their service, as she recommends; it feels like the polite thing to do. I got in the habit of folding and rolling storing socks and underwear. I pay more attention to whether my clothes still fit not only my body but my current life and personality.

Psyches as well as closets need to be decluttered, after all. Kondo vaulted onto bestseller lists in part because of her promise that tidying up—a term that, in my experience, comes nowhere near the effort required to deal with extreme clutter—conveys psychological and spiritual as well as material benefits. What the *New York Times* described as "this patting and hugging of belongings, a kind of compassionate organizing," made the tidying expert a sensation. Kondo has sold some 10 million books in 42 countries and regions, according to her website.

The Japanese-born Kondo's success reminds me of another, less sunny side of the history of decluttering: its associations with racism and anti-immigrant sentiment. As the 19th century wound down and the 20th century arrived, so did a flood of more goods, along with more people who might be tempted to buy them. Fresh waves of immigrants arrived in the United States and became part of an expanding, increasingly materialistic country.

In "How America Tidied Up Before Marie Kondo," a January 2019 *Smithsonian* magazine article timed to coincide with the Netflix show, journalist Jackie Mansky invokes the Progressive Era's "hygiene reformers, or home economists who advocated for a clean-living movement." Mansky cites the scholar Scott Herring, whose work examines how these mostly white, middle-class women pushed an agenda that linked a healthy, orderly domestic environment to being white, middle-class, and native-born and that viewed immigrants and people of color as messy, dirty, unhygienic. Clutter-busting thus became a way not just to improve one's own life but to signal racial identity and nativist virtue.

It's notable, then, that so many 21st-century Americans have turned to a foreigner for tidying-up advice. Hailing from another culture may work to Kondo's advantage: Greeting a house and thanking clothes for their service feel like exotic rituals to some Americans not familiar with the Japanese traditions Kondo draws on. And some observers have rightly detected whiffs of xenophobia and racism in both surreptitious criticisms (*How dare a woman of color set herself up as an expert?*) and public compliments (*She's so cute and perky!*) aimed at Kondo.

Whatever reactions the KonMari method generates, though, tolerance lies at the heart of its creator's appeal. If Kondo ever feels judgy about the volume of junk a client has accumulated, she does not show it. She's unflappable, respectful, sympathetic, never phased by situations that make viewers of her show gasp in shock or horror.

I wondered, as I watched, what she would have made of my mother's house. For me, and for many people, clutter sparks anger, anxiety, a fight-or-flight response. How soothing to encounter a decluttering professional who approaches the chaos of domestic life without judgment or reproach. Contrary to how most of the world reacts to extreme clutter, Kondo is... *nice* about it.

Maybe she's just plain nice. "What you see on TV is what you see in person," says Melissa Hagen Klug, a certified KonMari consultant based in the Minneapolis area who has met Kondo twice. "She just radiates that joy."

Given Kondo's popularity, you might expect everybody with an organizational bent to sign up to become one of her consultants. It's not that easy.

Klug was only the second person in Minnesota to become certified in the method. She belongs to a select group of organizers—more than 400 worldwide as of June 2020—who have made it through the rigorous certification process. She described the experience to me over the phone as she drove from

Minneapolis to visit a client in another state, a trip she makes often. (I thought of the traveling peddlers of earlier times.)

Would-be consultants must first apply the method to their own homes, submit before-and-after photos, and affirm that they embrace the principles involved. If aspirants make it through that stage, they enroll in a two-day intensive training course. (It is being offered virtually for the first time in 2020.) After she took the course, Klug did about 80 hours of work with practice clients and submitted reports to a team of reviewers, then took a test.

"The evaluators are really pretty tough," she said. Only about half of the people who take the training seminars go on to become certified, according to Klug.

In 2017, Klug founded her consulting business, Home by Eleven. Though she's Minnesota-based, she has regular clients as far afield as Iowa. She's worked with people as young as nine and as senior as seventy-five, but most of her clients are women in their thirties, forties, and fifties. From what she has seen, the emotional weight of clutter, and the pressure to do something about it, affects women disproportionately. "Whether you are the CEO of a company or a stay-at-home mom, the burden still falls on women," Klug said. "A lot of the women I work with just reach a point of 'I'm tired of coming home every day'" to the mess.

It takes not just organization sense but resilience and empathy to guide clients through the process of tidying. "It's such an emotional process for people," Klug said. "That's what I don't think anybody understands."

Her clients often describe themselves as overwhelmed. "They legitimately are so paralyzed they don't know where to start," she said. "I look at a pile and I see a Tetris game. They look at it and they see stress."

As a first step, Klug asks clients to tell her about their things and what they struggle with most. Some have visceral physical reactions; one woman began to sweat and breathe rapidly when she confronted her closet.

Many start telling stories. "It's not just stuff," Klug told me. "Every possession has some sort of emotional back story." Simple items—water glasses, a Jell-O mold—unleash stories about and memories of family dynamics.

Some messes are not easily tidied up, as I know first-hand. Organizers often become de facto therapists.

"Guilt and shame are the two biggest things I deal with," Klug said. A client may feel guilty when she gives away an item given to her by a relative; she might feel shame when she has to confront how much money she wasted on items she never wears or uses. "Even though these are not my things, it can be emotionally draining," Klug said. "I feel a lot of empathy for my clients."

That can take its toll on an organizer. Sometimes Klug needs to walk away and decompress. But the process of helping people makes it worth the emotional cost.

To get clients through the sometimes rough process of tidying up, KonMari organizers focus on what Klug calls the "guiding light at the end of the tunnel": What do they want their home to look like at the end of the process? Who do they want to be when they're done tidying?

When I dropped off a bag of clothes at my local second-hand clothes store in late 2019, the owner said she'd had seen an increase in donations and in new consigners since Kondo's book came out. Since then, she said, as customers browse the racks, "they'll ask 'Does this spark joy?'"

One catchphrase, or one consignment store in one city, does not a trend confirm, but Goodwill's numbers in early 2019 add up to more than anecdata. In the Washington, DC area, where I live, Goodwill received 66 percent more donations for the first week of January 2019 than it did for the same period in 2018, according to *The Washington Post*. One Gaithersburg Goodwill location saw an eye-popping increase of 372 percent.

Not all of those donations can be credited to a frenzy of Kondo-driven closet cleanouts. The federal government shut down for an extended period around the same time, and the many of the DC area's government workers found themselves with too much time on their hands. If they couldn't work, they could at least tidy up.

Like most vogues, this one experienced backlash. Some skeptics have mocked the idea of thanking inanimate objects for their service and wasting time on sock drawers. Others see Kondo's methods as either misguided or a threat to what they hold most dear.

In *The Life-Changing Magic of Tidying Up*, the author informed readers that she doesn't keep more than 30 books in her house. In one episode of the Netflix show, Kondo tells clients that they should hold each of their books and (surprise!) see whether it sparks joy.

Book-lovers roared with disapproval. Readers and writers wrote defiant tweets and columns in defense of their groaning bookshelves. Novelist Anakana Schofield vented her outrage in a caps-inflected tweet:

> Do NOT listen to Marie Kondo or KonMari in relation to books. Fill your apartment & world with them. I don't give a shite if you throw out your knickers and Tupperware but the woman is very misguided about BOOKS. Every human needs a v extensive library not clean, boring shelves.

Book critic Ron Charles (disclosure: he's a friend) has a houseful of books, which makes Kondo's advice unworkable for him, as he explained in a *Washington Post* column: "To take every single book into my hands and test it for sparkiness would take years. And during that time, so many more books will pour in. (How do you say "The Sorcerer's Apprentice" in Japanese?)"

Charles went on to describe a deeper cause of attachment to things—books, in this case, but it could apply to other categories of possessions as well. He observes that Kondo gives her TV audience the insight that de-accessorizing books "will show you what kind of information is important to you at this moment." His response? "We don't keep books because we know 'what kind of information is important to us at this moment,' he wrote. "We keep them because we don't know."

These strong reactions said more about the commenters than about the decluttering guru and her advice. In an interview with IndieWire, Kondo reassured bibliophiles that she did not in fact want them to toss their beloved personal libraries: "If the image of someone getting rid of books or having only a few books makes you angry, that should tell you how passionate you are about books, what's clearly so important in your life," she said.

Other critics felt an existential threat lurked behind the advice to whittle down one's belongings. Dissecting *The Life-Changing Magic of Tidying Up* in *Slate* when it first appeared, critic Laura Miller saw not order but a yawning void. "To discard the stuff we've acquired is to murder the version of ourselves we envision using it," Miller wrote. "Kondo's books constitute an insistent if oblique consideration of our own mortality, and the soon-to-be-departed, dear reader, is you. Death: the supreme life-changing magic."

To my mind, that's an overly negative reading. But an existential truth does lurk beneath any serious attempt to deal with a lifetime's accumulation: You really can't take it with you, even though consumer culture trains us from birth to believe we should acquire lots of "it" before shuffling off this mortal coil. To reckon with what will become of your worldly goods, you have to acknowledge that you will die. Surround yourself with All the Things; Death will still find you, sooner or later. You can't hide from the inevitable behind a mountain of stuff.

Material goods help ground people; they're vessels of history and identity. But they have a timeline independent of their current owners. However precious an object might be to you today, however much it carries in monetary or aesthetic or sentimental value, it might well outlast you by years, decades, even centuries.

More precisely, *you* will not be with *it*. Few people like to face the reality that many of the things that make up our daily lives, our memories, our family legacies, our inheritances, will last long beyond the point where we will be around to appreciate and enjoy them. Many of them were made or manufactured long before their current owners came into being and will be here years or centuries after they have died.

———————

As the self-appointed archivist for my immediate family, I try to project myself decades into the future, when my children have reached the age I am now. What books, documents, or photographs will be meaningful to them? I imagine that I will leave them a thoughtfully curated selection of the highlights of our family life, the best photos, the most significant school papers, the artwork that will reveal to their future selves the essence of who they were at five, ten, or fifteen. That's probably a fiction.

Still, this thought drives me to try: I do not want my children to have to spend a lot of time going through boxes of stuff. I don't want them to have to make a lot of painful decisions about what to keep and what to toss. I hope they'll have better things to do.

Given my family's history of having trouble letting go of things, it was a shock to me to discover that a cleanout doesn't have to be an ordeal. Swedish writer Margareta Magnusson makes the inevitability of parting seem downright cheerful in her slim 2018 book, *The Gentle Art of Swedish Death Cleaning*. Somebody has to deal with all of your things sooner or later; why shouldn't it be you? It might even be fun!

It's also an act of kindness. "Do not ever imagine that anyone will wish—or be able—to schedule time off to take care of what you didn't bother to take care of yourself," Magnusson writes. "No matter how much they love you, don't leave this burden to them." (In the margin alongside this passage in the book, I wrote "Thanks, Mom," with a frowny face penciled next to it.) Magnusson's subtitle—"How to free yourself and your family from a lifetime of clutter"—drives home the excellent point that "death cleaning" not only liberates the person who has acquired too much stuff, it unburdens their heirs and relations.

Putting the Swedish death-cleaning philosophy into action, neighbors of mine on Capitol Hill recently held a downsizing party as they got ready to move from the house they'd occupied for 41 years. They couldn't take everything with them to their new, much smaller condo. So they threw a party and asked guests to choose an item to leave with, and they told stories about each thing as it exited their lives.

"I've had to deal with the downsizing of my parents' home," one sixty-year-old guest told the *Washington Post* columnist Petula Dvorak, another Hill resident, who wrote about the event. "It wasn't easy. Something like this would've made it so much easier."

The painful cleanout of a family home has become a ritual of modern American life. I remember describing to a co-worker the situation I faced at my mother's house. It seemed outlandish to me; surely nobody else's parents managed to hoard as much as mine did.

A colleague about my age came in to refill his coffee and shared his own horror story about *his* mother's house. Another person came in and told *her* story of familial clutter, which included the discovery that her parents had at some point stopped opening their mail altogether; instead they stuffed it into garbage bags in the attic. She spent most weekends driving from DC to New York to go through all those bags and everything else squirreled away over the years.

At work and elsewhere, the cleanout stories piled up, tales of emotional as well as physical clutter. A friend described to me, over drinks, how she and her husband had taken off a week from work and showed up at her mother's house to insist on a cleanout and a reckoning with all the junk.

A scholar using the study shelf above mine at the library told me how her father, a schoolteacher, would bring his school papers home every year and deposit them in the basement of the family home. When she asked him what he intended to do with them, he told her it would be her problem.

And so it was, eventually.

Add all those individual stories together and they amount to a huge generational load. We deal with our relatives' stuff because we have to—somebody has to do it, right?—and because it's an act of love and caring or, sometimes, a purgative act, the dumping of old resentments along with everything else that's no longer wanted or needed. That so many people just shrug and shoulder the familial burden doesn't just speak to familial piety. We've normalized a state of excess that isn't normal.

The collective volume of so many things obscures the value of individual items that might otherwise be enjoyed by their owners and then treasured by heirs. "A loved one wishes to inherit *nice* things from you. Not *all* things from you," Magnusson writes. By the time you've cleaned out a house packed with someone's belongings, no matter how nice, most of those things come to feel like a burden or a curse, not a treasure or a blessing. I could not stop to read through all the notes and letters I found in my mother's files, or to browse through all her books, or recall and celebrate the professional accomplishments and personal milestones the clothes in her closets took part in, or puzzle out the histories of family trinkets whose stories were obscure to me even as a child and are now probably lost for good.

I had too little time for reverence and respect during the cleanout, focused as I was on just getting through the mountain of work required of me. I wish I had had the inspiration to do what a friend of mine did and use the online cataloguing service LibraryThing to create a record of her late mother's library. It was all I could do to get myself over to my mother's house weekend after weekend, month after month, and chip away at the accumulation. There was little time or energy left to celebrate, commemorate, or mourn the life she'd created and then abruptly had to leave behind.

I did find solace in dispatching my mother's things to good homes, or at least to places that would give them a chance to be useful again. I would have enjoyed the chance to consider more of my mother's things in their own right rather than as burdens to be disposed of.

In her book *Downsizing the Family Home: What to Save, What to Let Go,* Marni Johnson describes decluttering parents' houses as a generational rite of passage for contemporary Americans. As Boomers age, move into smaller places, or die, their Gen X and Millennial relatives are called on to step up and clean up after them.

And there's a lot to clean up in our elders' "fully loaded" houses. "The family home is loaded in every sense," Johnson writes. "It's loaded not only with belongings, but also with memories."

Like many other commentators I have read, Johnson sets the problem in the context of the postwar age of prosperity:

"After generations of relative scarcity and thrift, from the 1950s onward, this nation has experienced booming consumerism. A ready, steady supply of inexpensive household goods has filled homes—closets and cupboards, garages and sheds, attics and basements—to bursting."

Capitalism ginned up demand for those goods, industrial production manufactured the goods, merchants and advertisers hawked them to a public groomed for consumerism. Still, blame mostly gets assigned to the people who filled those closets and cupboards. A financial planner who specializes in downsizing tells Johnson that "Americans got too wrapped up in having things.... They bought into the culture of stuff."

The Great Recession, the planner says, "has helped them get back to quality, not quantity." Something has gone deeply wrong in a society where it takes a major economic blow to correct excessive consumerism, and where people now expect to be saddled, often at the busiest time of their lives, with cleaning up everything the previous generation could not or would not deal with itself.

Johnson observes that some aging parents deal with their own things; in her view, and in my experience, such people are exceptions to the general rule that *Hey, the kids will deal with it.*

This replicates, on a personal level, the shortsightedness and abnegation of responsibility that have handed us climate change. It's too much trouble to sort out all this stuff; dealing with it just reminds us that we're going to die anyway and that none of it matters. *Let the kids deal with it.*

Johnson, kinder than I felt when I had to step up to the task, approached the cleaning out of her family home of fifty years with a filial piety that would make an ancient Roman proud. In her book, she chronicles "the learning and loving and letting go" after she and her brother moved their parents into assisted living.

She also brought a reverence to the task that makes me shake my head in disbelief and a touch of envy. "Calling your parents' belongings clutter seems demeaning," she writes. "We're dealing with a vast amount of memory-laden, historical, occasionally valuable, often irreplaceable acquisitions. In short, we're talking about the museum of your family's life."

If I'd had a copy of *Downsizing the Family Home* when it was my turn, it might have helped me process the enormity of the task and feel less alone with it. My generation should probably be grateful for this cultural turn that recasts decluttering not as torture but as a cathartic, even (dare I say it?) fun process.

Still, Roz Chast summed it up best for me in *Can't We Talk About Something More Pleasant?* when she described how she felt about having to sort through her parents' lives: "I was sick of the ransacking, the picking over and deciding, the dust, and the not particularly interesting trips down memory lane."

All those whimsical phrases—"the pile of postponement," "Swedish death-cleaning," "tidying up"—don't change the essential mortal calculation, the net loss of time and energy required to clean out a family house. Behind the slogans, though, lies a long and rollicking debate about the best way to live—an ongoing push-and-pull that draws on pragmatism, aesthetics, spiritual practice and, now more than ever, sustainability.

CHAPTER 5

Waste, Want, and Wealth: Decluttering as Activism and Entrepreneurship

Not long after I finished cleaning out my mother's house, I went to hear a woman named Bea Johnson give a talk about the movement she's been spearheading. As its name suggests, the Zero-Waste Living movement seeks a radical reduction in what gets tossed and trashed, both by manufacturers and consumers. Adherents set out to produce as little waste as humanly possible.

While many decluttering experts emphasizes the quasi-spiritual aspects of eliminating excess, Zero-Waste Living focuses on the practical, environmental, and economic reasons to pare down. "Less stuff, more life," as a friend of mine likes to say.

Johnson staked her claim to fame on what most would consider an extreme form of minimalism: The amount of garbage she and her family produce in a year fits in a Mason jar. Her family includes her husband, two teenage sons, and a tiny dog that would have fit nicely into my mother's parade of pets.

I went into Johnson's talk a skeptic. The Mason-jar gimmick seemed just that—a gimmick. I came out persuaded, impressed, and a little daunted.

Johnson's California-based family buys what it can in bulk (even wine). They bring reusable containers to the grocery store. They compost nearly everything (including the bamboo handles of their toothbrushes) and make do with what most contemporary Americans would consider an absurdly limited amount of stuff for daily living.

Their frugality extends to fashion as well. Johnson owns 15 pieces of clothing. I think of my mother's overstuffed closets and conclude that less might well be more.

The budgetary and ecological benefits of Zero-Waste Living should be obvious. There's a catch: It requires considerable time and effort to live this version of the simple life. Johnson has found a full-time job—and a lucrative career—in streamlining how she and her family live.

Of course Johnson has a book, *Zero Waste Home: The Ultimate Guide to Simplifying Your Life by Reducing Your Waste*, which I bought after her talk. (So much for minimalism.) "In the manufacturing world it engages cradle-to-cradle design," she writes. "In the home it inspires the consumer to act responsibly."

By "responsibly" Johnson does not mean putting those cans and cereal boxes in the recycling bin. She calls recycling "a last resort before the landfill." She prefers what some call "precycling," although she does not use that term. If you don't buy it or bring it home in the first place, you don't have to recycle it or otherwise get it out of your life.

Better to say no to them in the first place—to refuse, in the parlance of the Zero Waste movement's 5-Rs mantra. Johnson describes the 5-R approach as "five easy steps": "refuse what you do not need; reduce what you do need; reuse what you consume; recycle what you cannot refuse, reduce, or reuse; and rot (compost) the rest."

The first step—"Refuse"—requires a shift away from the take-the-freebie mentality that's become the norm. But it takes less effort to say no to a tote bag than it does to reduce your household waste to fit into a Mason jar. Skip the swag at the conference, the free mini shampoo bottles at the hotel, the paper receipt at the store: If enough people say no, the collective impact could be substantial.

"Every bit we accept, or take, creates a demand to make more," Johnson writes. "While the individual act of refusing does not actually make the waste disappear, it creates a demand for alternatives."

———————

Corporate actions carry far more weight than individual ones, however. Trader Joe's recent decision to cut back on the amount of plastic it uses in its stores will make a greater dent in our collective over-packaging problem than my new habit of saying no to single-use plastics.

Such refusals add up to "just bottle caps in an ocean" of plastic, as the journalist Ashley Wicker observed in a May 2019 article in *Vox*. "Since 2010, the fossil fuel industry has poured $180 billion into new plastics manufacturing facilities, and experts say global plastic production will jump by 40 percent as a result, irrespective of whether we bring mason jars with us to the grocery store."

Wicker's *Vox* article deals head on with one aspect of a bigger question I had been grappling with: How big a role does gender still play in the quest to declutter, organize, and live more harmoniously with our things?

Women like Bea Johnson and Marie Kondo have carved out substantial shares of the broader organizing/decluttering/sustainable-living market, but men still dominate the minimalist movement. There's Joshua Becker, the founder of the "Becoming Minimalist" empire of books, podcasts, and newsletters. Joshua Fields Milburn and Ryan Nicodemus, aka The Minimalists, "help over 20 million people live meaningful lives with less through their website, books, podcast, and documentary," according to their website. Press opportunities abound for these high-profile mavens: "The Minimalists have been featured in the *New York Times*, *Wall Street Journal*, *Boston Globe*, *Forbes*, *Time*, ABC, CBS, NBC, FOX, BBC, and NPR."

Now as ever, the push to declutter relies on female labor to get the word out and the job done. That's nothing new. William Morris got to be the visionary aesthete/designer; Isabella Beeton and the Beecher sisters wrote instruction manuals, hundreds of pages of detailed advice on how to keep home and family humming along. The fight against clutter has long been female.

There are exceptions. In my family of origin, my father tended to be the organized one, albeit with a scholar's tendency to accumulate research materials. But most of the passionate talk I've heard about organizing and decluttering, whether at home or at work, comes from women.

In most of the families I'm acquainted with, women serve as the organization police. They're the first responders when a clutter crisis hits. They (we) are more likely to notice when the domestic sphere has become taken over by an excess of stuff. They (we) are more likely to take action to do something about it, sometimes to the annoyance of partners and offspring. Sometimes the male-identifying members of households pitch in, but they are less likely, in my experience, to take charge of a decluttering mission. I've encountered category exceptions, for instance when it comes to who organizes tools and garages. But organizing at the most basic household level trends female.

In Wicker's analysis, the Zero Waste movement falls largely to women to spearhead. It perpetuates and extends the persistent Second Shift phenomenon, in which women labor all day at paid work and then come home to another round of unpaid work they're expected to shoulder. Now they're supposed to tackle the ecological crisis while doing it, as Wicker writes:

> It's essentially another layer to "having it all": a career, a family, a perfectly Instagrammable life, and now you're saving the planet, too. In practice, this can be a

lot of undervalued, unpaid work, more added to the "mental load" that women carry, which ... is the list-making and calendering that women do to administer the household.

Whoever does it, a zero- or lower-waste lifestyle requires a fair amount of planning and preparation up front. To move effortlessly through a zero-waste workday means you have to head out loaded for bear, by which I mean equipped with an arsenal of items and tactics designed to get you through the daily routine of the average American consumer-worker without giving in to the single-use plastics and disposable everything the modern American system runs on. I jotted down a list:

- Reusable water bottle (plastic, metal, or glass)
- Reusable utensils (metal, heavy-duty plastic, or bamboo)
- Reusable straw (probably metal, usually accompanied by a pipebrush-style cleaner to scour out the remains of your smoothie or iced drink)
- Reusable tote bag for any shopping you might need to do
- Reusable containers (e.g., Mason jars) or bags in which to store grocery items you might need to buy

That's not an exhaustive list of everything you could carry with you, but it's a pretty good start. In the age of manbags and backpacks, men might easily carry all these items with them.

But many men and some women (like my teenage daughter) still prefer what Wicker calls the "keys-wallet-phone" approach. If they want to do the sustainable thing, they need to carry an extra bag. Women used to schlepping purses or work bags can accommodate a zero-waste kit more readily.

Do all this and you still have to navigate a retail world ill-prepared to deal with customers who want to reduce waste. At many stores, especially the larger chains, clerks have to be convinced that, no, you really don't want or need a plastic bag or a receipt for your purchases. Most of the big grocery stores, in my area anyway, haven't yet added bulk-purchase items for shoppers who want to cut back on plastic packaging when they buy beans, flour, and other pantry staples.

For a working person on a tight schedule and budget, zero-waste living still requires more preparation, more stops, and the emotional and social labor of having to deal with perplexed store clerks. Unfortunately, many of the alternatives to Zero Waste Living also depend on disposable income.

For instance: Have too much stuff and not enough time to deal with it? Buy more stuff to store it in.

Since its founding in 1978, the Container Store has dangled the promise of stylish organizational salvation in front of American consumers. Clothes, photos, kitchen items, gift wrap: Almost any category of object a modern household needs to store meets its match at the Container Store. Buy the right storage container and tame the clutter at last. (Never mind that it defies logic to deal with too much stuff by buying more stuff.)

Marie Kondo advises her fans to repurpose shoeboxes and other ready-to-hand items as storage solutions. She's not a minimalist, nor does she advocate zero purchases; in 2019, she opened her own online store. But the decluttering mania she helped stoke has been good for the storage-solution business.

For the fourth quarter of fiscal year 2018, which ended March 30—well after Kondo's Netflix show aired—the

Container Store announced that its consolidated net sales had hit $253.2 million, a jump of 8.8 percent over the fourth quarter of the previous fiscal year. In a press release, the company's chief executive officer, Melissa Reiff, attributed the growth not only to its ongoing efforts to improve and expand its offerings in stores and online but to "the positive impact from 'the Marie Kondo effect' that is driving even more interest in our core category of Custom Closets and storage and organization."

Another persistent fixture on the organization landscape has been the glossy magazine *Real Simple*. It predated the KonMari phenomenon by a decade and a half and has persevered as other glossies foundered and readers turned for advice to reality TV shows and minimalist podcasts.

Founded in 2000, it parlayed its get-organized philosophy into a branded constellation of better-living and storage products. *Real Simple*'s 2020 media kit claims that the magazine has a print reach of 7 million readers, and that its audience is 90 percent female (no shock there), with a median age of 52 and a household income of more than $100,000. These are affluent readers, then, mostly upper middle class, in the middle of their lives, mid-career and/or mid-parenting. They want sensible advice on how to live the kind of domestic life the magazine's photo spreads promote: "easier, more beautiful, and more meaningful," as the *Real Simple* mission statement puts it.

That sentiment flirts with the spiritual side of decluttering, but the magazine itself defaults to homey, nonthreatening, easily managed advice. A browse through the "Organization" section of the website turns up comforting listicles heavy on words like "pretty" and "practical." I sense a relentless cheerfulness in all this, as if the magazine had been taken over by that can-do parent in the carpool who always whips up a batch of brownies for the school bake sale.

Consumerism drives the agenda. The secret to an organized life a la *Real Simple* appears to be *Buy more things*: a rolling tool cart for the garage, maybe, or a set of cute storage cubes for the home office. Lulled by the lovely photo spreads and the domestic fantasy they serve up, one could forget that *Real Simple* would not exist if it did not attract advertisers willing to pay $270,000 for a full-page ad. That business model has to move products if the magazine wants to stay in business.

———

One way or another, there's decent money to be made off the decluttering craze. Contemporary female entrepreneurs, like their Victorian counterparts, have seized the opportunity. If Isabella Beeton of *Mrs. Beeton's Book of Household Management* fame were alive today, she might be an investigative journalist—or a member of the largely female National Association of Productivity and Organizing Professionals (NAPO).

The association began in 1983, founded by a group of organizers in LA; now it has about 30 local chapters and some 3,500 members, most of them women. NAPO offers a Certified Professional Organizer credential, putting a professional stamp on what's long been considered part of the traditional female skill set, but many members set up shop as personal organizers without that certification.

Although professional organizers don't charge corporate-lawyer rates, their hourly fees—which can range from $35 to $125 or more, depending on the region, the client, and the amount of experience an organizer brings to the work—are nothing to sneeze at. If you enjoy organizing stuff, like working with people, and want a flexible schedule, you could do a lot worse for employment.

Anybody who has worked in the cubicle farms or open-office plans of modern offices will understand the appeal of working from home, on your own schedule. So will anybody who has experienced sexism, ageism, racism, or other discriminations rampant in the workplace. If the tech-bro culture of Silicon Valley startups or the high-stakes world of venture capitalism shut you out, you can build a viable business on your own schedule, for very little overhead.

A century and a half after Mrs. Beeton took the domestic world by storm with her bestselling how-to book of household management, professional organizing has turned a traditionally unpaid female skillset into a contemporary business opportunity. It generates income, offers flexible hours, and carries no penalty for being, say, a middle-aged woman with family responsibilities. It is today's equivalent of what Realtor training offered women of my mother's generation. It validates and monetizes duties that women have long been expected to embrace: tend to the spaces in which daily life unfolds.

Many organizers work first as subcontractors for other organizers who have jobs big enough to require a team of people. Some organizers consider themselves paperwork specialists; some focus on offices; some work primarily with seniors and downsizers, others with families with young children.

Whatever their specialty, organizers are having an extended moment. People still joke about retail therapy and how a little shopping would do wonders to lift a bad mood or banish a bad day. But decluttering is the new shopping, a pick-me-up that feels virtuous in part because of the transformative promise it holds out. Life-changing magic indeed.

On one of the sullen, hot, and humid days that distinguish summers in the DC area, I took a long Metro ride out of the city to the suburbs of northern Virginia to meet professional organizer Debbie Smith. A member of NAPO since 2016, she's now the president of the Washington, DC chapter of the organization.

We met at Tyson's Galleria in Tyson's Corner, one of the region's main commercial hubs. Most of whatever greenery used to be there has been razed and replaced with sleek malls and glass-heavy office towers. The whole place stands as a temple to shopping, business, and the automobile. To be a pedestrian there feels transgressive and more than slightly dangerous, as I discovered on my 10-minute walk from the Metro station to the mall.

With Debbie, though, I felt right at home, even though the suburban terrain made my urbanite self feel out of place. Blonde and cheerful, Smith comes across as the kind of upbeat and easygoing person you'd be glad to count among your relatives or see at your college reunion.

Smith is in her early sixties. Like many professional organizers, she switched careers well into her working life, after stints in airline security and insurance sales. Within a few minutes of meeting her, I could tell she has the knack of putting people at their ease, a skill that comes in handy if you're a professional organizer. Because, as with almost everything involving clutter, it's not just about the stuff.

"I find the most important quality a professional organizer can have is emotional intelligence," she told me, echoing KonMari consultant Melissa Klug. "You do really need to be sensitive to people's moods and backgrounds. You become a bit of a therapist."

Smith favors a flexible approach tailored to each client. She doesn't insist that everyone begin with a certain category like clothes and move from there through a prescribed series of categories. Instead she picks what's likely to be the easiest starting point for a client traumatized or overwhelmed by the magnitude of the task ahead. Recently she helped a client and her husband downsize from a 25-room house to one half the size. She described the process as one of persuasion, not prescription:

"I said 'Let's start with the room you use the least. Then, in this month while you're moving, you can get some feel for how this process works," she said. "Separate what you want to donate, what you want to sell, what you want to keep, what you want to throw away. And once you get that going, you're going to feel confident. It's going to make you feel like 'Okay, I can do this.'"

The client's husband told Smith that when he'd leave the house in the morning, his wife would be in tears as she contemplated the work ahead. When he came home at the end of the day, he'd find his spouse laughing with Smith as they worked. As anyone who has had to deal with clutter can tell you, the burden of it lies not just in the volume but in the emotions attached to it and to the prospect of dealing with it.

The secret to decluttering success, from a professional organizer's point of view, is to help the client find an even keel amidst the chaos. "It's not just about getting the things out of the house," Smith said. "It's about emotionally and mentally not feeling overwhelmed and drowning—and maybe even enjoying it."

That works with the majority of clients. But the chronically disorganized and those with hoarding disorder require different approaches. According to Smith, few professional organizers work with hoarders; those cases require interventions and skills that go beyond what NAPO members or Kondo's army generally do.

"Hoarding is a medically diagnosed mental challenge, and you need to have extensive background and additional training if you are working in a true hoarding situation," Smith said. "If you're not properly trained, experienced or prepared, you can really do more harm than good," she said. "It's a frustrating and challenging field to work in and most organizers don't get satisfaction or joy out of it."

For clients with chronic disorganization, a good decluttering and setting up of sensible systems won't be enough to keep them organized. Those clients tend to relapse and to need periodic check-ins or tune-ups from a pro organizer, according to Smith.

Such clients are sought after by organizers, because they can be good long-term sources of income, but they present frustrations too. If you're an organizer, Smith says, "you're a list maker. You love to cross things off that list… It's an incredible feeling to have someone say 'Can you organize my garage? Look at this garage. Empty it out." And you put it all back together perfectly in six hours. It's such a sense of satisfaction for you and the client. But when you're working with a chronically disorganized person, you're never going to get there."

Professional organizing appealed to Smith both because of her temperament—she's always been an organizer, the family historian, at home with project-management tasks—and because of her background. She grew up in a military family, which meant they never stayed too long in any one place. "I was a Navy brat. We moved every 18 months, and my mom was very organized. She had to be. It really holds."

Smith's mother, now in her nineties, at one point had to muster four kids under the age of five, which must have been a military-style logistical operation in its own right. When you don't stay in any one place too long, you don't have much opportunity to accumulate too much stuff. You get used to culling papers and belongings on a regular basis.

I think of my own parents, who lived or still live in the same houses for decades. Forty or fifty years in one place gives you a lot of time to accrue papers and books and clothes and furniture and souvenirs and tools and artwork and more, with little imperative to cull or de-accession. Nothing forces a decision about what's worth keeping like knowing movers are about to descend on the house.

Unlike some professional organizers, Debbie Smith does not resent Marie Kondo. "She has put organizing on the front page," Smith told me. "She's done so much for our industry to publicize it."

I asked what some pro organizers don't like about Kondo's approach. "They think she's saying this is the only way to do it," Smith said.

As she sees it, you don't have to be a full-on Kondo devotee to find useful inspiration in the method. "You always learn either something you don't want to do or something you could do better."

This mix-and-match approach doesn't have catchphrase electricity. But given the infinite variety of people and their attitudes toward their stuff, pragmatic flexibility makes sense for organizers on the front lines of domestic clutter.

Even as they adapt what they do to clients' particular circumstances, productivity-and-organization specialists follow certain best practices, according to Heather Cocozza. She's the founder of Cocozza Organizing & Design LLC and serves on the executive board of NAPO.

Cocozza comes out of the corporate world, with extensive experience in project management at PricewaterhouseCoopers and IBM. Now she and her company provide organizing and productivity services to residential and business clients. I met her at a Starbucks in northwest Washington, DC, to hear more about her work.

In person, Cocozza comes across as warm, helpful, and well prepared. It was easy to picture how she could help a stressed-out client deal sit down and sort through a backlog of files decades in the making. Like many organizers, she started with individual clients who needed a hand with home organizing; she now works with many institutional clients as well, including a major museum complex.

It surprised me to learn that the two realms—home

and workplace—offer similar challenges from an organizer's perspective. Cocozza found the transition easy to make. "I was already in people's homes and their home offices using this best-practices system, so I didn't have to rewrite anything," she told me. "I just did the same thing I was doing, but could apply it at a larger scale."

Cocozza credits two now-classic books on organization as inspirations for her approach: *Organizing from the Inside Out* by Julia Morgenstern and *Taming the Paper Tiger* by Barbara Hemphill. The basic strategy makes a lot of sense: Set up a sensible, sustainable system of higher-level categories and sort, label, and discard accordingly.

"A typical breakdown at home would be your financial records, your lifestyle records, your vital records," she said. "If you had a business, your business records would be separate."

If this sounds straightforward, consider the multitudes of distractions that arise over the course of an average day, week, or month. A professional organizer will not only set up a system but coach the client on how to set aside time to maintain it.

"Most of the people I work with come to me because there are one to three things they really want to do, and they just can't find the time," she said. "They're frustrated."

As I heard from other organizers, the job also requires an appreciation that people often have strong feelings that get in the way of moving ahead. Cocozza works with many clients in the midst of a transition: an office reorganization, for instance, or a retirement. Forty years' worth of office files represents a life's work as well as an organizational challenge. To sort through them requires emotional fortitude and trips down memory lane, not unlike confronting a cache of family snapshots and memorabilia.

Digital files and systems make up an ever-larger part of Cocozza's workload, although contemporary offices and homes still contain many paper tigers in need of taming. One big challenge created by digital files, Cocozza told me, is that they often belong to systems used by multiple employees or divisions. For a shared digital system to work, all parties who use it have to be on board and agree on labels and categories. Chaos arises spontaneously; order needs a helping hand.

———————

As NAPO's membership has grown, so has the amount of organizational self-help advice out there. Welcome to the era when a self-described happiness researcher can build a career on the kind of get-it-together wisdom your best friend might drop over a glass of Chardonnay.

I first heard Gretchen Rubin on an episode of "Stand Out," NAPO's podcast, which focuses in part on how to run a small business. I mention Rubin not to single her out in particular but because the advice she dispenses—via books and newsletters and her own podcast, "Happier with Gretchen Rubin"— captures the tone and style of mainstream organizational-and-productivity thought these days.

On the NAPO podcast, Rubin offered advice so sensible it was just about argument-proof. I listened to the episode while running on the treadmill at the gym and found myself nodding in agreement.

Can't bear to clean out all your closets at once? Start with half a shelf and work from there. [Okay.] Are you sunniest when surrounded by a bounty of well-curated items? There's no shame in abundance—a favorite word of Rubin's—if it's mindfully selected. [Makes sense.] Worried by a boss who believes a clean desk signals an organized mind? Take comfort in knowing that maybe you're one of those creatives who needs a certain amount of stuff around you to do your best work, whatever your minimalist-minded boss says. [Been there.]

People must respond to this kind of advice, because I had to wait to borrow Rubin's recent book *Outer Order, Inner Calm: Declutter & Organize to Make More Room for Happiness* from my local DC Public Library branch. It represents the latest installment in her ongoing investigation of how to lead a happier life, a project that has (so far) produced five books (not counting her books on other subjects, including Winston Churchill and JFK), 275 podcast episodes as of late May 2020, video courses, workshops, and more.

Was the book worth the wait? *Outer Order, Inner Calm* itself turned out to be a brisk, soothing 215-page read. I found it hard to disagree with almost anything in it—and if I hadn't written down some quotes, I'd remember almost nothing about it. "In the context of a happy life, a messy desk or a crowded coat closet is a trivial problem—yet getting control of the *stuff* of life often makes it easier to feel more in control of our lives generally," Rubin writes.

Love Kondo's method or hate it, you probably have an opinion about it. The innocuous nature of Rubin's advice makes it hard to remember. Instead, Rubin offers her readers a sensible-sister's rubric for making decisions. "When trying to decide the fate of a possession, ask yourself: *Do I need it? Do I love it? Do I use it?*"

———————

How did people get so busy, so overwhelmed by the avalanche of consumer goods that they keep all these advice mavens and organizational experts in business?

I have a running list of theories: The obsession with clutter, and getting rid of it, gives people a way to reconnect with the world of objects at a time when life feels ever more digital. People organize and declutter to distract themselves from the seriousness of living in the Anthropocene and its existential threats—a burning planet, the Sixth Great Extinction, killer plagues, nukes in the hands of rogue states, the collapse of liberal democracy, the disintegration of civil society, and the rise of demagogues at home and abroad. Decluttering and practice minimalism work as a collective sort of self-soothing, inoculating us against the pandemic of anxiety that has swept the United States. Not to mention that sometimes it's fun to dump all your clothes on the bed and re-imagine who you are and who you want to be.

All of these theories point toward the same conclusion: The never-ending war on clutter represents a hunger to find or create order out of the unpredictable chaos of life. Whoever's peddling it, much of the contemporary advice on how to live an organized (and therefore happier) life targets individuals and their habits and choices.

I see a bigger and more dangerous agenda at work as well: An organized life boosts productivity, the holy grail of American life. Get organized and you will become a more efficient economic cog in the engine of late-stage capitalism.

At home, decluttering your living space will make you a more productive member of the domestic team; it will free up your valuable time and limited energy to shop or carpool or cook those important family dinners. At the office, clearing your desk turns you into a better, more efficient employee who will get more done and generate more profits for your employer.

Often, in the gig economy, that employer will be you. NAPO's members, after all, are small-business owners, the essence of the American entrepreneur. Remember that the "P" in NAPO stands for "productivity." To get to the promised land of productivity, at work or at home, requires an immense amount of time and energy and labor—and most of it is still female.

I asked Debbie Smith of NAPO why the majority of professional organizers are women. "I think it's a DNA thing," she said. "Women like to figure things out, men like to fix things." Maybe, she said, that division of labor is hardwired; maybe it's how we were raised.

In September 2019, at Smith's invitation, I went to the fall kickoff meeting of NAPO's DC chapter. Of the 80 or so attendees—a record turnout, I was told—about 70 were women. Most of the men there worked as junk haulers or antique dealers, and came to the meeting in their capacity as business partners of NAPO members.

After a catered dinner and some networking, the attendees got to hear from Susan Kousek, a longtime certified professional organizer who specializes in time management. Making decisions "is a major, major problem for many of our clients," Kousek told us.

Manage your time well and you stay organized; let that executive function slip, though, and things fall apart. She reminded the audience that organizers now need to be aware of mental health issues and disorders that clients might have: ADD, ADHD, chronic disorganization, hoarding disorder.

Productivity took top billing, though. There was a strain of "Organizer, organize thyself" to the presentation. "Productivity is closely related to time management," Kousek said. That applies to organizers as well as to their clients. "If you're self-employed and you're wasting time, you're only hurting yourself," she said.

As I chatted with some of the organizers after the meeting, one theme emerged: Most of them came to clutter-busting via personal ties. They got their start as organizers helping friends and family clean out closets or downsize when the time came. They discovered they were good at it. They enjoyed helping people. Several had regular office jobs and set up organizing businesses on the side, then transitioned into full-time entrepreneurship as their client base grew and/or they left other jobs and careers.

In our conversation, though, Debbie Smith made it clear that the people skills necessary to be a successful organizer can create tricky ethical and personal questions. Is a client paying an organizer to deal with disorganization or to be a de facto friend and confidante?

Because the work can be so personal, taking place as it often does in people's most intimate spaces, in bedrooms and closets and other spaces where people store hide secrets, amid things they can't bear to part with but also might rather not confront, a personal organizer must balance compassion and a personal touch with a resolute setting of boundaries. If a situation calls for skills or training that a particular organizer lacks, it's time to refer the client to someone else.

When I think of my mother, and the relatives of friends who have had to tackle major cleanouts, and the people on Marie Kondo's show and on *Hoarders*, and all those who turn to personal organizers for help, I'm struck by how many people want—need—some kind of outside intervention or assistance to get unstuck. We're drowning in the byproducts of a system that makes productivity a priority and encourages people to be consumers first and foremost. This is the way of the modern world: Get, get rid of, repeat.

Unfortunately, the "get rid of" part of that equation is a lot more complicated than making a Goodwill run or calling the junk hauler.

CHAPTER 6

Final Destinations:
Clutter as Junk
and Eco-Catastrophe

As I've pointed out throughout this book, clutter feels personal. Books, articles, and TV shows routinely treat or exploit it as individual failing: *What are you going to do about all this junk you've accumulated?*

For a long time, I blamed my mother alone for her situation. Those truckloads of clutter Frank hauled away represented decades of poor decision-making, a useless stockpile of goods built up over years by unwise financial and emotional choices. Once I'd cut through the clutter—when I was at last free to set my mother's case alongside other consumer histories big and small—I began to see she was not altogether the author of her own disaster.

Individual decisions, habits, and neuroses matter. Nobody forced my mother to buy many dozens of high-end shoes or hundreds of cookbooks. But it's a lot harder to resist things when you're embedded in a culture that shouts "Buy!" at you, through multiple megaphones, over and over and over again, decade after decade. To dump all the blame individual consumers ignores the net of economic structures and imperatives in which those consumers make decisions.

It also ignores a question that gets more pressing every year: How should we reckon with the life cycle of all that stuff we manufacture, ship, buy, store, and discard? Inconvenient and disturbing as the thought is, all the goods that crank through and rev up the modern consumer economy come from somewhere—many somewheres—and in the end they have to go somewhere.

The system that makes it so hard for consumers like my mother to have a healthy relationship with what they buy has produced a number of interim solutions to the overabundance it pushes. Those who can't cram everything into their houses or apartments can turn to the $38-billion-a-year self-storage industry, which maintains some 2.311 billion square feet of rent-a-space in more than 50,000 facilities across the country, according to a 2018 story in *Curbed* magazine. Shop, click, and store.

A lucrative peer-to-peer side business has sprung up: renting out storage space in your house or garage for other people's clutter. "Airbnb for inanimate objects" is how a 2019 *Guardian* story on the phenomenon described it.

This to me sounds like hell, given the struggles my family has had to contain and store its own extraneous objects. But as the *Guardian* noted, several startups now facilitate such storage sublets: Stashbee in a number of UK cities, Costockage in France, Stashii in Canada, and Australian startup Spacer, which has expanded to the United States.

Spacer offers a clearinghouse for parking spaces to rent. But it also offers listings for attics, basement storage rooms, and other suitable spots in which to dump your detritus until you can deal with it. Spacer's founder, an Australian named Mike Rosenbaum, told *Business Insider* Australia that he was inspired by the sharing economy in which services like Airbnb and Uber had flourished. He has ambitions for Spacer to become "a global marketplace of space," taking advantage of what he described as a worldwide trend toward smaller living quarters. "So the biggest problem is where do you want to store your stuff?"

I did a search for available storage space in the Sydney area, where Spacer is headquartered, and learned that for $480 AU a month, I could rent the second bedroom in somebody's flat—just to stow stuff, not to live in. For $1,500, I could rent an entire basement for my things, with access during weekday business hours and on Saturday mornings from 8 to 12. (More tempting, if a little unsettling, was a "book and wine storage box" in New South Wales for about $9/month, with a promise that the facility would not inquire into the contents of said box.)

Whatever the price range, the Spacer model fits into the sharing-economy model often associated with the Millennial generation but increasingly familiar to those older and younger. No need to go through the hassle of owning it if you can rent it, whether it's a car or a place to stow your gear. This strategy can go hand in hand with a push to accrue fewer possessions in the first place; then again, if you have an affordable space in which to stow any overflow, you put off an honest reckoning with how much you own.

That reckoning has to come, sooner or later. This is where the system that created modern clutter really breaks down.

It would be better for consumers and the planet if we had Henry Mayhew-style street sellers in 21st-century cities. In DC, we have Goodwill and AMVETS (American Veterans), curbside single-stream recycling, and city-sponsored depots where residents can drop off compostable food waste. There's Frank with his pink dump truck, and the big junk-hauling enterprises like 1-800-GOT-JUNK. Washingtonians make use of self-storage units (not cheap) and Craigslist and neighborhood listservs like Nextdoor and my local Capitol Hill parents' group. Unwanted bookcases, chairs, lamps, and kitchenware still find their way to the city's curbs, usually (but not always) carried off within a few days. Little Free Libraries have popped up on many of the blocks within walking distance of my house, and the public library branch still valiantly puts out and empties its blue book-donation bin every day.

But the outflow of unwanted items far exceeds the outlets ready to absorb and rehome or repurpose them. Nobody is going to come down my street with a cart or a wagon and buy our outworn or outmoded clothes, unwanted household furnishings, and other residential castoffs that might still have life left in them.

The contemporary United States hasn't abandoned scavenging. A healthy industrial secondhand trade still exists, documented in a deep-dive, Mayhew-worthy 2019 piece by Jake Halpern for *The New York Times Magazine*. Halpern made the rounds in Buffalo and its suburbs with a professional scavenger named Adrian Paisley, who goes prospecting for copper wire and tubing and other industrially valuable materials trapped inside discarded appliances, pianos, and other discards. China now turns away US plastic and paper, but it hungers for scrap metal as it ramps up industrial production and depletes its own resources.

Halpern describes the abandoned industrial buildings of Rust Belt cities like Buffalo as a sort of city-scale clutter:

> With so many products now manufactured overseas, countless factories are deserted, and many of the malls and retail stores we once patronized are also shuttered. In short, we have a glut of garbage from the objects that we have discarded, but we also have the derelict infrastructure that once made and sold this stuff.

Contemporary scavenging feeds off industrial America's discards. Scavengers like Paisley, and the larger scrapping outfits he sells to, have found a way to put some of this architectural clutter back into circulation.

"Over time, scrappers have remade Buffalo's landscape. The city has survived, in part, by devouring itself," Halpern writes. "Starting in the late 1990s, as China's demand for metals increased, there was suddenly an incentive to demolish and scrap Buffalo's derelict houses, factories and industrial machinery." It wasn't just pianos and air conditioners being scavenged and salvaged but shuttered steel mills and auditoriums.

More than half a million people work in the scrap industry, according to statistics Halpern obtained from the Institute of Scrap Recycling Industries. "That exceeds the number of Americans who work as computer programmers, web developers, chemical engineers and biomedical engineers combined."

It's not crazy to think that if we can scale up the scavenging trade to the level of whole buildings, we could also shrink it down to neighborhood size again. Imagine how the balance of use and reuse could shift away from the binge-and-purge mindset toward sustainability. Somewhere out there is a contemporary Henry Mayhew waiting to chronicle it when it happens.

In the meantime, we remain stuck with imperfect and partial systems of reclamation and recovery. In spite of the current mania for it, decluttering feels like a lonely pursuit, not like part of the vast economy of recycled, repurposed goods that Halpern describes. Decluttering pits owner versus things in a contest of will versus inertia. What is the declutterer who wins the battle supposed to do with the spoils?

My preferred if imperfect method, depending on what I'm parting with, is the curbside-treasure approach: I set the unwanted item on the curb out front with a sign that has "Free!" scrawled cheerfully across it. If it's an appliance or piece of electronics, adding a reassuring "Works fine!" sign can help nudge the undecided off the fence and into carting the thing away.

People will take almost anything if it's free. I sometimes lurk by the window in hopes of catching someone in the act of acquisition, especially for more unlikely items. You'd be surprised—or maybe you wouldn't—at what gets snapped up.

Over the years, we've gotten rid of lamps, bookshelves, a chaise longue with a wonky leg but a lot of comfortable sitting left in it, all manner of toys and party favors, books, CDs, candlesticks, boots, even a box of refrigerator magnets that I collected on work trips over the years and that over time lost whatever appeal they'd had when I snapped them up at airport gift shops. I put a box of them out on the curb, not really expecting anybody to take them, and by the end of the day the box was empty. Nothing beats free.

This grassroots system also provides a test of how people who don't know each other conduct transactions that don't require them ever to meet. In the absence of a "Free!" sign, it can be hard to tell whether an item really has been put curbside as a giveaway. A neighbor of mine put a box of garden hoses on the curb while she awaited the moving truck; someone carted it off, likely unaware that the hoses weren't actually up for grabs.

A bigger downside of the curbside economy's usefulness is that it is too easy to pick up as much as or more than you discard. The outflow from my house still exceeds the inflow, but only barely.

But who could resist a perfectly good patio umbrella for the table on the back deck? How can someone who lives with piles of books on the floor say no to another sturdy bookshelf? My husband has learned to dread texts from me alerting him to my latest find, which he likely as not will be called on to strong-arm into the back of the car. Once in a while the item, whatever it is, has to be strapped to the roof, it's so big. I'm especially proud of those finds and the heroics required to muscle them home.

Many of those freebies have been useful, some wind up again on the curb, but true need only sometimes drives the acquisition. But they're free! What good consumer could say not to a bargain like that?

The clutter-to-curb cycle doesn't suit all environments. It requires a certain residential density to function at its best. It's a system that works best for denizens of cities and well-populated suburbs.

In a rowhouse neighborhood like mine, there's enough foot and vehicular traffic to provide a stream of potential takers for most of the items a household like ours is likely to give away. The more distance between dwellings, the less chance someone will happen by and cart off a chaise longue.

The rise of the internet has given the giveaway economy a boost. The Capitol Hill parents' listserv we've belonged to for years serves as a virtual bazaar in which goods are swapped and sold. Many days, most of the message subject lines begin with "FREE" or "FS" (for sale). People give away baby togs and sporting gear, pantry items like raspberry-leaf tea, hydrangeas and azaleas displaced by landscaping work, vintage hallway tiles, even breast milk. Those in search of specific items—coffee cans for school projects, empty moving boxes, second-hand bikes, unused chargers for old computers—post almost as often, and often find what they're looking for. It's a satisfying mix-and-match carousel of goods, a moving river of stuff that flushes clutter out of space-constricted houses and puts items back in circulation. Some items go through multiple owners, hand-me-down hand-me-downs. Henry Mayhew would appreciate the economy of it.

If the listserv doesn't locate a home for a particular item, the internet offers a vast platform for giveaways. The nonprofit Freecycle Network, for instance, works like a virtual curb on which to put unwanted items for people nearby who might want or need them.

Founded in 2003, Freecycle anticipated the current wave of interest in sustainability by a good fifteen years. The nonprofit says it now has more than 9 million users worldwide, clustered in more than 5,000 local groups. Its mission statement hits all the right sustainable-living notes: the goal is to create "a worldwide sharing movement that reduces waste, saves precious resources & eases the burden on our landfills."

Even Freecycle is not a space protected from the buy-more message that dogs us everywhere we go. As I browsed the Freecycle site, a pop-up J. Crew ad appeared to urge me to buy a dress, with the promise that my closet would thank me. (My wallet would not.) I tried not to dwell on the irony that a site devoted to the sharing economy depends partly on ads that encourage fresh consumption.

I have never been a big user of Freecycle but have spent time trawling the WANTED and OFFER listings posted in the DC group. So many things on offer, an abundance that fills me with wonder and despair. So much time and labor and money went into producing and purchasing all those goods, and more time and energy goes into the managing of them. Still, I should be glad they're not landfilled or dumped in the woods somewhere.

———————

What the curbside-treasure approach and Freecycle can't absorb often ends up carted off to big donation-driven enterprises like Goodwill. Long before the KonMari craze, Goodwill runs had become a staple of weekend life for many American families, including mine. Most of the year round, my family keeps a bag or box near the front door to collect outgrown clothes and unwanted odds and ends; when we have a critical mass, out it goes to the local thrift store.

Ritual household cleanings have an ancient history, and many of us still undertake a big spring or fall effort to sort out our domestic affairs. It's a kind of ritual purge of clutter whose modern final act involves bagging it all up and donating it—or making it someone else's problem—in the name of charity.

While Goodwill doesn't scream religion, it owes its existence to a socially conscious Boston Methodist minister, the Rev. Edgar J. Helms, who founded "America's Original Thrift" in 1902. Helms's philosophy of "a hand up, not a handout" applies to Goodwill Industries today, which offers job training and employment to people in need.

In theory, then, Goodwill provides a guilt-free way to de-accession unwanted stuff. Donors take comfort in thinking that those too-small Converses and outmoded jeans won't end up landfilled, like the 12.8 million tons of textile waste that Americans dumped in the trash in 2013.

Every time I took a carload of my mother's discards to my local Goodwill, though, I'd look at the mountain of random donated goods piling up at the collection point and wonder: Where does it all go, really? (I am hardly the first to ask. The question of why and how we dump unwanted things has even spawned an academic cottage industry devoted to what we get rid of and why we get rid of it: "discard studies.")

Goodwill takes all manner of goods, but it can't and won't take every item. Junk haulers, though, will take almost anything you're willing to pay to have out of your life.

With his trash-hauling business, Junk in the Trunk, Frank Coyne has something in common with the Victorian street-sellers of yore, at least in terms of entrepreneurial spirit. Like them, he helps close some of the gaps in the lifecycle of consumer goods. But the economics of the exchange have shifted, and now consumers pay to have their discards carted away rather than being paid for them.

Frank's an easygoing, easy-to-laugh guy in his forties with two kids in school and a long-standing client base that means he doesn't have to hustle for jobs. Long ago, he was in financial services, working on an MBA, but he got fed up and quit. He got involved in junk hauling almost by accident. He had a pickup truck and started making runs to the city dump on weekends to get rid of construction debris from a fixer-upper he owned.

"I found myself going to the dump on weekends to take demo debris from my house, and there were the same guys there every time who looked like they were making a living doing it," Frank told me when we met at a local coffee shop to talk about his adventures in the junk trade.

At first, he said, persuading people to pay him money to haul their stuff away was a hard sell. Almost two decades later, he's got a thriving business—and the aches and pains to show for it. "It's a good living," he says. "It's very hard on my body. But I think we do pretty well."

Frank's company occupies a boutique niche in an industry dominated by franchises like Junk King and 1-800-GOT-JUNK, whose familiar blue trucks race to the scenes of clutter crimes in "Hoarders." The smaller scale of Frank's operation allows him to take more time to sort and process what he hauls away; clients call him in part because they know he tries to donate and recycle everything he can.

When you book a visit, Frank and a couple of his regular helpers show up in a dented but sturdy pink dump truck. (I asked if the truck has a name. It doesn't.) Frank books the jobs and does most of the talking while the crew works calmly and efficiently, loading the pink truck with impressive geometrical precision. No nook or cranny goes unfilled. Then they haul the load to one of the area's trash-and-recycling depots, or transfer stations, for sorting and discarding.

When they helped me clear out my mother's house, Frank and his guys worked with the discretion of undertakers—appropriate, given that the task felt funereal to me. They did not comment on the state of the house or the depth of the mess. They picked up and packed up with respect and without question. All of that made a hard job easier.

Later, in a calmer state, I asked Frank how bad my mother's house really was. Surely it ranked among the worst he'd seen.

"Oh, no, it wasn't bad," Frank said, in his typically kind way. He described houses where stuff stacked floor to ceiling made it impossible to walk through any room, houses where he and his crew found carcasses—opossums, dogs—under the detritus as they worked to clear it. My mother's clutter, catastrophic as it felt to me, didn't make the top 10, maybe not even the top 100.

A cleanout requires muscle as well as tact. Frank and his crew spend most of each day hauling, lifting, and unloading almost every kind of item that might wind up being thrown out at homes and offices. Tables, sofas, mattresses, books, records, pots and pans, old appliances—you name it, the Junk in the Trunk gang has probably hauled it away. They can't take everything; hazardous materials require special handling and disposal, and Frank doesn't want to put his crew at risk.

The day-to-day hauling is hard on a body. Think back to the last move you did yourself and how you felt the next day. Then imagine doing that kind of heavy lifting all day, every day, over and over. This is also part of the price that clutter exacts.

"Until a couple of years ago I was, I kid you not, maybe taking 25 Advil a day to make it through the day," Frank told me. "Early on it was fine. You know, it was stupid of me. I was like 'I feel so strong, this is great and I'm making money.'"

Now he reminds the crew to slow down and pace themselves. He's gotten more careful about what jobs he takes on and what he won't haul away—construction debris, for instance. "We don't do dirt anymore," he said. "We don't do concrete. We try to stay away from pianos and hot tubs now." That's reduced the aches and pains, but cumulative injuries still linger.

He wonders whether the asthma he developed a few years ago is related to the particulate matter he breathed in when the company still carted away construction debris. Frank didn't use face masks then. "Now we're really good about it, but the damage is done," he says.

There's emotional heavy lifting to reckon with as well. Frank and his crew have to be respectful at all times when dealing with clients. They know the process of cleaning out a house can trigger strong emotions.

Frank understands that and sympathizes. Some clients need to take a minute, or many minutes, to deal with memories stirred up by items bound for the pink trunk. But he's also got a schedule to keep, and often has multiple jobs to get through on a given day.

"It's tough when you walk into a home and you don't know the personalities, and you have a job scheduled in three hours," he says. "There's always this kind of tension, like if you say the wrong thing, if you do the wrong thing, is there going to be tears or anger?"

There are times when he'll get a call, days or weeks later, from relatives who wants to know what happened to a specific item some other family member sent packing. Some of them imagine Frank has a warehouse where he stores what he hauls away. (He does not. The scale of the operation would make that unworkable, even if he wanted to keep stuff, which he doesn't.)

With just me to deal with, Frank said, he and his team had it fairly easy in terms of decision-making. Other times they find themselves in the middle of a family feud about what to keep and what to toss.

He recalls a small item of furniture—a side table, maybe—that one sibling kept telling him to put on the truck only to have another sibling come up and tell him to take it off again. "Then a third sibling popped up, and this went on, and at the end there was some backroom screaming," he says. "A lot of siblings, they've never gotten along. And especially in a moment like this, they disagree about every little thing."

He remembers a job he'd slated two days for. "We got there and this woman just couldn't handle it," he says. Screaming and tears followed. She sent the crew away.

It turned out that the woman's family had made plans for the cleanup without informing her. "This was their fault," Frank says. "They thought that was the best way to deal with it."

In the past five years or so, though, Frank has noticed a sea change. He and his crew have had fewer encounters with distressed clients and extreme clutter. He attributes that to the rise of personal organizers and downsizing experts, who not only sort through accumulated stuff but manage personalities and emotions throughout the process.

"Now they're first responders, and we're just sort of the backup," he says. "We're still doing all the heavy lifting, but they do the emotional heavy lifting now."

The challenges don't stop once everything has been loaded on the pink truck and the client is out of the picture. Frank's team does their best to sort out the recyclables from the things that cannot be salvaged. (In the junk-hauling business, this sorting out is sometimes called "landfill diversion.") But there's no guarantee that increasingly overwhelmed consignment stores and nonprofits will take furniture or other still useful items, even if they're good quality.

There's an art to loading the truck so as not to waste any space and, just as important, to maximize the chances that items won't be landfilled. The best items— those sturdy or valuable enough to interest consignment stores and nonprofits—go on the truck last, in hopes that the decision-makers at Goodwill or AmVets or A Wider Circle will see them first and say yes to them. "These charities are so busy, there's so much stuff people are getting rid of," Frank says.

One place he takes donations keeps an enormous compactor out back, into which they dump perfectly good items they can't sell and don't have space to store. Frank doesn't judge them too harshly. "I'm sure they do as good a job as any of salvaging stuff, but I guess you can't save it all."

When the Junk in the Trunk crew loads up the truck, they sort everything so that it can travel safely, first to consignment stores and then to be offloaded at one of several municipal transfer stations in the DC metro area. Those stations too are feeling the pressure of the rising tide of discards.

Over Frank's time in the business, some of the closer-in stations have closed as developers look for prime urban and suburban parcels to develop; the remaining depots have gotten pickier and/or have raised the fees they charge junk haulers. Some have added surcharges for couches and mattresses. That adds up if you've got a small truck.

Lines and wait times have gotten longer, too. "The lines are so long, everything is so slow, everything gets piled up," Frank says.

In spite of the best efforts of organizers, junk haulers, and consignment store staff, many discards will not find a useful second life, nor will they be recycled. With nowhere else to go, they'll wind up in landfills. What began as an individual, local problem then morphs into a national or international one.

A few years ago, on a short flight for a business trip, I sat next to an engineer who talked about how much energy has been buried in landfills, waiting to be tapped by the engineers of the future. In the shorter term, though, landfills are the result of a wasteful system that produces more than society knows how to use and re-use.

According to the American Society of Civil Engineers (ASCE), Americans produce about 258 million tons of what's known as municipal solid waste, or MWS, every year. The ASCE estimates that about 53 percent of that gets dumped in landfills, 35 percent is recycled, and 13 percent is incinerated to produce energy.

Those numbers mean little to someone in the throes of a cleanout, caught up in the stress and pressure of what's often a tough situation. I remember one overwhelming feeling by the time I called Frank in to help: *Just get it out of here.*

I also remember the guilt-tinged relief of watching the pink truck drive away, loaded with things that no longer were my problem. Once discarded stuff gets loaded on the junk hauler's trunk, it might as well not exist. But exist it still does, somewhere. To treat clutter as an individual or family problem, as this culture long has, means putting off a larger reckoning.

"There is a need to change the way we think of how solid waste is generated, managed, and potentially used as a resource," the ASCE writes in the solid-waste section of its 2017 Infrastructure Report Card. "We need to recognize that what is routinely discarded may in fact be a reusable resource."

Many people think of clutter as a burden that just weighs down domestic spaces, a plague of stuff confined to basements, garages, attics, and home offices. But the plague has spread far beyond the limits of individual lives and homes. The landscape-level clutter of billboards and unplanned suburban sprawl, for instance, creates crowded and chaotic environments that replicate on a huge scale the conditions many consumers contend with at home.

At the broadest level, the appetite for more stuff has cluttered up the planet in ways that humans have not yet reckoned with—in spite of its urgent consequences. The environmental consequences of fast fashion, for instance, have been well documented.

Fashion doesn't shoulder the responsibility alone. The

production and shipping of mass-market consumer goods eats up resources that ecosystems can no longer spare. The spread of the culture of convenience has created a throwaway mentality that junks up the planet. (See the #plasticapocalypse hashtag on Twitter for a stream of real-time examples.)

All those disposable cups and straws—and everything else that gets tossed—wind up somewhere. Landfills, like storage units, create temporary solutions that don't solve the bigger problem of what to do with all the junk.

The Great Pacific Garbage Patch has gotten a lot of press in recent years, for good reason. The name invokes, wrongly, a floating continent of plastic, derived from Asia and the western coast of North America by ocean currents that carry it thousands of miles. The National Oceanic and Atmospheric Administration (NOAA) and *National Geographic* describe it as more of a soupy mess of waste than a solid island of garbage.

However visualized, the Patch represents clutter on a grand scale, a symptom of the price extracted for the cheap things we keep making, shipping, and buying, with high environmental costs at every step of the process.

In June 2019, the *Guardian* newspaper debuted an investigative series that it called "United States of Plastic." The first installment reported on the export of America's plastic waste, much of it collected as curbside recycling. The United States "generates 34.5 million tons of plastic waste a year, enough to fill the Houston's Astrodome stadium 1,000 times," according to the *Guardian*'s analysis. Much of that went to landfills, but about 1.6 million tons used to be shipped to China and Hong Kong for recycling. (The thought of the bottles and containers my family puts out in the blue recycling bin every week being loaded up on container ships and sent across the ocean staggers me.)

In late 2017, China closed its doors to much of America's plastic waste because of contamination. "Since the China ban, America's plastic waste has become a global hot potato, ping-ponging from country to country," the *Guardian* wrote. "America is still shipping more than 1m tons a year of its plastic waste overseas, much of it to places that are already virtually drowning in it."

The pictures that accompany the series show nightmarish scenes of plastic bags, bottles, and other detritus that overwhelm workers and communities in Thailand, Vietnam, Cambodia, the Philippines, Turkey, and elsewhere, smothering villages, covering beaches, producing an environmental disaster that threatens to eat up the world. A system that creates such waste and then quite literally dumps it an ocean away is a system dangerously out of balance.

You do not have to be a Zero Waste practitioner to know by now that recycling has serious limitations, both as an answer to clutter and as a way to save the planet from the toll of overconsumption.

With the market for recyclables in doubt, the media began to scrutinize what many Americans, after many municipal efforts at education, had come to accept as a normal and virtuous practice. In the summer of 2019, for instance, a crew from Chicago's WGN TV rode along with a Republic Services recycling truck making the rounds in the suburb of Oak Park, where residents are active recyclers. Some 20 to 25 percent of what's collected can't be recycled. "Wish-cycling"—committed by well-meaning people who try to recycle inappropriate items like Styrofoam—is partly to blame.

So is basic human sloppiness. "Food waste, liquid waste—believe it or not, we get a lot of diapers," a Republic Services rep told WGN's reporter. That kind of cross-contamination means that a lot of would-be recyclables have to be landfilled.

The Atlantic's Alana Semuels neatly encapsulated the problem in a March 2019 story about how the recycling crisis has made it prohibitively expensive for many US municipalities, which used to be able to sell the recyclables they collected, to keep their programs alive. In Franklin, New Hampshire, for instance, the town manager told Semuels that recyclables were now being incinerated instead of shipped off for processing: "We are doing our best to be environmentally responsible, but we can't afford it."

A lot of US recyclables, then, have become clutter—too much stuff with no clear purpose. This pressure on recycling comes at a time when the United States is creating more waste than ever. According to Semuels' reporting, in 2015 "America generated 262.4 million tons of waste, up 4.5 percent from 2010 and 60 percent from 1985. That amounts to nearly five pounds per person a day. New York City collected 934 tons of metal, plastic, and glass a day from residents last year, a 33 percent increase from 2013." And that was before the COVID-19 pandemic of 2020 quarantined New Yorkers and the rest of the country at home, generating yet more waste (single-use gloves, wipes, etc.) and recyclables (takeout containers, delivery boxes) and putting pressure on already strained waste-disposal systems.

Think of the number of tote bags, water bottles, and other swag handed out at conferences, distance races, school and job fairs, and store openings, part of the branding juggernaut we've long been accustomed to. A few tote bags come in handy, especially in a city like DC that has imposed a 5-cent tax on plastic shopping bags. (The funds go to cleaning up the Anacostia River, where many of the area's plastic bags used to wind up.)

Still, the global story of where all the discards go turns out to be more complicated than the familiar narrative of wealthy nations dumping all their junk on poor ones. Adam Minter has spent a lot of time documenting the global river of secondhand goods—everything from shoes and clothes to e-waste—that flows from more affluent to less affluent US households, across national borders, and from continent to continent.

A journalist and Bloomberg Opinion columnist now based in Malaysia, Minter hails from the Midwest. He grew up in Minneapolis, the scion of a family that owned scrap yards. His immigrant great-grandfather got his start in the United States as a scavenger, part of a long tradition of rag-and-bone men everywhere.

Like me, Minter wondered where all that Goodwilled stuff goes. Early in his book *Secondhand: Travels in the New Global Garage Sale*, he recalls making a Goodwill run in Hopkins, Minnesota, to donate his late mother's china. Like me, he wondered where those donations would ultimately wind up. Was his faith that the china would be reused in some way justified? *Secondhand* follows Minter's investigation of what turns out to be an astonishingly complex and global system of exchanges.

For many discards, Goodwill turns out to be a waystation on a long journey. In *Secondhand*, Minter describes in richly reported detail how entrepreneurs and fixit men in Ghana and Malaysia and many other places have built a dynamic 21st-century version of the economy of reuse that thrived in Victorian Britain.

Broken or damaged TVs, computers, and cars get refurbished and reassembled or broken down for useful parts in Ghana. Secondhand clothing and shoes bought in bulk at US Goodwills by enterprising traders find new wearers across the border in Mexico. On and on, around and around it all goes.

The authorities generally don't love or encourage this "circular economy." Minter calls out the racism and colonialism behind restrictions that developed nations place on what discarded material get shipped where, and to whom, limits often imposed in the guise of protecting the less fortunate. As he points out, some of those restrictions end up doing more harm than good by keeping still-usable materials out of the hands of people who could actually do something with them.

Minter also calls attention to a phenomenon that contributes both to clutter and to waste: The quality of many consumer items has declined. That limits their longevity and the likelihood they will be repurposed. For instance, cheap clothes tend to be cheaply made clothes; they wear out sooner and don't make good rags later. That creates more waste along the ever-shorter road from closet to landfill. (Fast fashion comes at a high cost for workers and the environment too.)

Consumers can and should buy higher-quality things if possible—and keep them longer. "The best thing you can do is buy less stuff," Minter told NPR host Terry Gross when she interviewed him on *Fresh Air*.

Minter's reports from the global secondhand and recycling trades make a compelling case that, for the health of the planet and its inhabitants, the repair-and-reuse mindset needs to become universal again. "Use it up, wear it out, make it do or do without," as the old adage recommends. That mindset could help reshape the system in a way that allows us to live more gracefully, and gratefully, with the things we need, the things we cherish, and the things that make us happy— without destroying our budgets and the planet in the process.

EPILOGUE
The Changing Landscape
of Clutter

Cleaning out my mother's house drove home the realization that almost anything—clothes, cookbooks, evening gowns—turns into clutter once it is no longer used or cared for. In her attic, I found a weather-stained box of love letters my father wrote her when she was studying abroad in Austria and he was at Oxford. The letters, along with my mother's old straw basket with paintbrushes and palettes, a few small pieces of furniture, and other odds and ends wound up in a storage unit behind my own house. Some decisions I just couldn't bear to make, though someone eventually has to.

In the end, many of my mother's things wound up carted away to the landfill. Her books, though, were another story. My mother's extensive library—self-help, cookbooks, fiction, books on music and decorative arts, and more travel guides than I could count—filled up more than 60 cartons. I gave dozens to the local library, dropping them batch-by-batch in the blue collection box to feed the next Friends of the Library sale. My husband and I rented a van to drive the rest across the Potomac River to a woman who would sell them to raise money to buy books for schoolchildren. In contrast to the truckloads of discards I dispatched to local landfills, this mass migration of books felt like rehoming, not discarding. Freed from their limbo in my mother's house, I hoped, they would find new readers and come alive again in human hands.

Rehoming an excess of possessions takes far more effort than buying them in the first place. I worked hard to find new homes for anything that seemed still useful. A carload of office supplies went to the animal shelter. Thirty boxes of Italian shoes, along with my mother's working wardrobe and her evening gowns, went to a charity that helps people who need a fresh start in life. The same charity hauled away a truckload of furniture, including the dining-room table, two beds, three dressers, a desk, bookshelves, and dozens of boxes of kitchenware and household furnishings. Charities these days can afford to be picky, and they stay busy. I had to book a pickup time two months from when I called.

"We didn't realize there'd be this much," the leader of the crew told me when pickup day finally arrived. He did not seem pleased.

Towards the end, once I accepted that the house too had to go, the realtor we were working with found an estate-sale company that swoops in and does pop-up sales. But it somehow felt worse to sell my mother's things—the fine gilt-edged china, the sturdy platters I recall from long-ago holiday dinners—than it did to donate them.

At the bitter end, the day before the house sale went through, I still had about 2,000 LPs stacked in the living room. I advertised them on the neighborhood listserv—free to anyone who could come that evening and take them away. A few minutes later, someone pulled up in a Prius and loaded all the records into her car for a vinyl-loving friend who owns a brewery. Maybe, I thought, he would actually play them.

My mother's house was empty at last.

My battle with clutter did not end when the house sold. For me—and for the rest of the modern world—the war on clutter has no end in sight.

Clutter has long been a physical problem, but now it has colonized the digital world as well. In this tech-heavy age, digital content—emails, Word documents, photos, and more—piles up as clutter that's mostly invisible. As this new variety accumulates, though, it weighs people down just as much as its tangible cousins do. Call it virtual heavy contents.

In 2018, British researchers in the psychology department at Northumbria University published an early study of digital hoarding behaviors. They found their subjects experienced "themes common to physical hoarding ... related to the over-accumulation of digital materials, difficulties in deleting such materials, and feelings of anxiety relating to this accumulation/difficulty deleting."

Technology enables and entraps its users. I wouldn't call us image hoarders, but my husband estimates that together we have some 40,000 digital photos in our family archive, with more added all the time. We are not alone.

The longer I put off dealing with all those photos, the more anxious I get when I think about it. Almost everyone who uses smartphones and computers regularly will know the feeling. The age of the iPhone feels like one endless opportunity to capture everything, or drown in digital files trying.

I used to make time to sort through each year's photos and star the best ones, with the aim of creating a digital series of highlights or albums. The number of photos quickly outpaced the time and energy I had to sort through them.

How many photos does one person or family really need, anyway? Some shots wind up posted on social media or shared via online photo platforms with relatives and friends. Most of these impromptu photo archives will wait forever for someone to sort, tag, and organize them. I have lost count of the older relatives and friends who meant to get around to their own backlogs of analog photos in their retirements and (surprise!) never found or made the time. If they couldn't get make it through hundreds of photos, the digital-photo crowd stands even less chance.

People are too busy snapping more photos. *Business Insider* estimated in 2017 that humanity would take 1.2 trillion photos worldwide that year—a hundred billion more photos than the year before, most taken on smartphones.

Those images get uploaded in a flash to Instagram or another social-media platform. They're like potato chips, meant to be enjoyed in the moment.

All this photographic clutter creates new opportunities for anxiety (*What will I do with all these photos?*)—and yet more business opportunities (*I can't do this alone!*). Images now have an association devoted just to managing them: the Association of Personal Photo Organizers. The words that jumped out at me on the APPO website capture two essential components of clutter in any form: "abundance" (such a deceptively optimistic word) and "chaos."

Information comes at us in digital form all day long. Email gets lost in overstuffed inboxes; the phrase "Email is broken" has been uttered in countless offices. Documents pile up on hard drives and in Dropbox folders and Google Drive. Text messages and notifications stack up. A few years ago, the *Washington Post* writer Brigid Schulte even wrote a book, *Overwhelmed*, about how we're all swamped all the time and how bad it feels.

As with physical clutter, the world abounds in productivity experts who promise to help us tame digital clutter. Sites like the "Simplify Your Digital World" blog share tips on how to cut through the excess. Inbox Zero acolytes take a boot-camp approach to getting their digital lives in shape, though others have described this as yet another form of procrastination. This personal and collective cognitive overload constitutes a species of clutter too. Historians including Harvard's Ann Hood have documented how information overload is not new; people 400 years ago felt overwhelmed too, especially once printing came along. It's all relative—but the Internet and digital media amplify the problem. I expect it to get worse as the digital side of modern life expands.

Whatever forms the clutter of the near- and long-term future take—including digital and ecological—we'll need a collective mind shift to deal with it. Marie Kondo's popularity depends partly on her reassurance that in a society overwhelmed by things, it's still possible to find balance between too much and too little.

Can we make that shift? Can we make do with fewer but more meaningful things and take better care of the things that matter most—including the planet?

This is how I interpret William Morris's rule: Learn to *see* objects again, either because they serve a purpose (you know them to be useful) or for their own sakes (you believe them to be beautiful). Define use and beauty: Does an object matter because of its associations or because of what it can do? What does possessing it cost in time, money, or mental and environmental health?

Think about the hidden costs and histories of things. Everything has an origin story, some happier than others. Clutter gets in the way of the fact that things do matter—on a planetary and a personal level.

When the job of clearing out my mother's house fell to me, I felt overwhelmed, angry, and utterly unprepared. It was the hardest work I have yet had to undertake—physically, logically, and emotionally. Yet somehow, like so many of my generational peers, I got through it, because I had to. The more I got rid of, the easier it became to get rid of even more.

Unencumbered by stuff, my mother now lives in a small, uncluttered room at an assisted-living facility, surrounded by a few of the family pictures and objects I guessed would mean the most to her. She never asks about the house.

In the process of dismantling her life, I recovered some lost things: bits of family material history, and a richer sense of who my mother was, or had tried to be, over the years. As I decided what to keep and what to toss—a fascinating and fearsome process in its own right—I came to think about some familiar objects in a different way, and to appreciate them as souvenirs of lives led even as I made the decision to give them away.

I also experienced a version of phantom-limb syndrome: The weight of the things I discarded still haunts me now and again. At times it feels as though I didn't get rid of those things at all. Lodged in my mind, those absent-present objects preserve some essence of my mother as she used to be.

It reassures and unsettles me to have learned that while people are more than possessions, those things may persist in memory long after they have exited our lives. Like everything I have learned in the course of writing this book, I count it as another argument for being conscious about what to keep and what to save—to choose what matters enough to live with throughout a life, not just what to discard at the end of it.

I have promised my children I won't leave them the material mess that fell to me. I have to try. We all do.

BIBLIOGRAPHY

Arnold, Jeanne E. et al. *Life at Home in the 21st Century: 32 Families Open Their Doors* (Cotsen Institute of Archaeology, 2012).

Birchall, Elaine, and Cronkwright, Suzanne. *Conquer the Clutter: Strategies to Identify, Manage, and Overcome Hoarding* (Johns Hopkins University Press, 2019.

Briggs, Asa. *Victorian Things* (Sutton Publishing, 2003; first published by B.T. Batsford, 1988; revised for a Penguin edition, 1990, and a Folio Society edition, 1996).

Chast, Roz. *Can't We Talk About Something More Pleasant?* (Bloomsbury, 2014).

Chin, Elizabeth. *My Life With Things: The Consumer Diaries* (Duke University Press, 2016).

Cohen, Lizabeth. "A Consumers' Republic: The Politics of Mass Consumption in Postwar America" (*Journal of Consumer Research*, 31(1), 236-239).

Cohen, Lizabeth. *Household Gods: The British and Their Possessions* (Yale University Press, 2009).

Davis, Fanny Waugh. "A Housekeeper's Symphony" (*Good Housekeeping*, Vols. 44-45, 1907).

Dickens, Charles. *Our Mutual Friend.* Edited with an introduction by Stephen Gill (Penguin, 1971; reprinted 1983. First published in serial form in 1864-5 by Chapman and Hall, London).

Douglas, Mary. *Purity and Danger: An Analysis of the Concept of Pollution and Taboo* (Routledge Classics, 2002, with a new introduction by the author; first published by Rutledge & Kegan Paul, 1966).

Flanders, Judith. *Inside the Victorian Home: A Portrait of Domestic Life in Victorian England* (W. W. Norton, 2003; first American edition 2004).

Freinkel, Susan. *Plastic: A Toxic Love Story* (Houghton Mifflin Harcourt, 2011).

Frost, Randy O., and Steketee, Gail. *Stuff: Compulsive Hoarding and the Meaning of Things* (Houghton Mifflin Harcourt, 2010).

Gosling, Sam. *Snoop: What Your Stuff Says About You* (Basic Books, 2008).

Hale, John. *The Civilization of Europe in the Renaissance* (Atheneum, 1994).

Herring, Scott. *The Hoarders: Material Deviance in Modern American Culture* (University of Chicago Press, 2014).

Hothouse, Christopher. *1851 and the Crystal Palace: Being an account of the Great Exhibition and its contents; of Sir Joseph Paxton; and the erection, the subsequent history and the destruction of his masterpiece* (John Murray, 1850; revised edition, with introduction by Osbert Lancaster, published by Butler & Tanner, 1950).

Homes, Edward. *Garbology: Our Dirty Love Affair With Trash* (Avery, 2012).

Howard, Vicki. *From Main Street to Mall: The Rise and Fall of the American Department Store* (University of Pennsylvania Press, 2015).

Institute for Challenging Disorganization. *Clutter-Hoarding Scale: A Residential Assessment Tool* (Institute for Challenging Disorganization, 2011-2019.)

Johnson, Bea. *Zero Waste Home: The Ultimate Guide to Simplifying Your Life by Reducing Your Waste*, (Scribner, 2013).

Johnson, Steven. *The Ghost Map: The Story of London's Most Terrifying Epidemic—and How It Changed Science, Cities, and the Modern World* (Riverhead/Penguin, 2006).

Kondo, Marie. *The Life-Changing Magic of Tidying Up* (Ten Speed Press, 2014).

Kondo, Marie. *The Life-Changing Manga of Tidying Up* (Ten Speed Press, 2017).

Kondo, Marie. *Spark Joy: An Illustrated Master Class on the Art of Organizing and Tidying Up* (Ten Speed Press, 2016).

Leonard, Annie, Fox, Louis and Sachs, Jonah. "The Story of Stuff" (movie produced by Free Range Studios and released in 2007).

Le Zotte, Jennifer. *From Goodwill to Grunge: A History of Secondhand Styles and Alternative Economies* (University of North Carolina Press, 2017).

Licence, Tom. *What the Victorians Threw Away* (Oxbow Books, 2015).

Lidz, Franz. "The Paper Chase" (*The New York Times*, October 26, 2003).

Lippincott, Lorilee. *The Simple Living Handbook: Discover the Joy of a De-Cluttered Life* (Skyhorse Publishing, 2013).

Magnusson, Margareta. *The Gentle Art of Swedish Death Cleaning* (Simon & Schuster, 2018).

Mauriès, Patrick. *Cabinets of Curiosities* (Thames and Hudson, 2019).

Mayhew, Henry. *London Labour and the London Poor: A Cyclopedia of the Condition and Earnings of Those That Will Work, Those That Cannot Work, and Those that Will Not Work*. Dover Publications, 1968; unabridged reproduction of the 4-vol. work as published by Griffi, Bohn, and Company, 1861-62, with a new introduction by John D. Rosenberg.

Mayhew, Henry. *The Morning Chronicle: Survey of Labour and the Poor: The Metropolitan Districts, Vol. I-VI* (accounts published in 1849-50; Caliban Books edition, 1980).

McCarraher, Eugene. *The Enchantments of Mammon: How Capitalism Became the Religion of Modernity* (Harvard U. Press, 2019).

Minter, Adam. *Junkyard Planet: Travels in the Billion-Dollar Trash Trade* (Bloomsbury, 2013).

Minter, Adam. *Secondhand: Travels in the New Global Garage Sale* (Bloomsbury, 2019).

Morris, William. *Hopes and Fears for Art: Five Lectures Delivered in Birmingham, London, and Nottingham, 1878-1881* (1882).

Nicholson, Shirley. *A Victorian Household* (Barrie & Jenkins, 1988; Sutton Publishing, revised edition, 1998).

Obniski, Monica. "The Arts & Crafts Movement in America" (*Heilbrun Timeline of Art History*, The Metropolitan Museum of Art, 2000–).

Paxton, Matt. *The Secret Lives of Hoarders: True Stories of Tackling Extreme Clutter* (Perigee, 2011).

Plotz, John. *Portable Property: Victorian Culture on the Move* (Princeton University Press, 2008).

Rotskoff, Lori. "The Victorian Martha Stewart" (*The Women's Review of Books*, May-June 2007).

Rubin, Gretchen. *Outer Order, Inner Calm: Declutter & Organize to Make More Room for Happiness* (Harmony Books, 2019).

Sanborn, Jason. "America's Clutter Problem" (*Time Magazine*, March 12, 2015).

Schama, Simon. *The Embarrassment of Riches: An Interpretation of Dutch Culture in the Golden Age* (Fontana, 1988).

Schor, Juliet B., and Holt, Douglas B. *The Consumer Society Reader* (The New Press, 2000).

Sennett, Richard. *The Craftsman* (Yale University Press, 2008).

Siniawer, Eiko Maruko. *Waste: Consuming Postwar Japan* (Cornell University Press, 2018).

Trentmann, Frank. *Empire of Things: How We Became a World of Consumers, from the Fifteenth Century to the Twenty-First* (HarperCollins, 2016).

Vaidyanathan, Siva. "The Decade in Advertising: Targeted Ads Exploded, and the Damage Has Been Devastating" (*Slate* magazine, December 27, 2019).

Viewing, Gerald, and Mendes, John, eds. *Exchange and Mart: Selected Issues 1868-1948* (David & Charles Reprints, 1970).

ACKNOWLEDGMENTS

This book belongs to a much bigger conversation about how we live with things, a conversation carried on and continually expanded by journalists, historians, psychiatrists, social workers, organizing experts, and many others. I could not have written it without their research, experiences, and insights, which I have tried to credit both within the text and in the bibliography. It's a rich and growing body of work.

Many people who work with clutter, one way or another, were generous with their time and expertise, including Capt. Andrew Brown, Dr. Gregory Chasson, Heather Cocozza, Frank Coyne, Melissa Klug, Dr. Tom Licence, Dr. Jennifer Sampson, Debbie Smith, and Dr. Susan Strasser. I am grateful to them for sharing their insights and experiences with me.

On a more personal level, I want to thank everybody who confided their own clutter stories as I worked on this book. Those stories—sometimes funny, sometimes achingly sad—reminded me that while clutter is easy to turn into a joke (so many "spark joy" headlines!) or reality-TV fodder, it is a painful and intimate subject. Hearing other experiences of clutter and cleanouts helped me appreciate the emotional depths and complexities involved—and feel less alone in the struggle.

This book wouldn't exist without the wonderful publishing team at Belt Publishing. My talented editor, Dan Crissman, understood from the beginning why I wanted to write about clutter; he encouraged me to move beyond a journalistic take and grapple with the heart of the matter. I am deeply grateful to him, and to Anne Trubek, Belt's founder and publisher and editor/writer extraordinaire, who encouraged me to send the proposal to Dan.

Many friends saw me through the highs and lows at every stage: Louis Bayard, my coffee-shop writing buddy; Meredith

Hindley, who brings history to life; Marie Arana, Susan Coll, Dana Elfin, Gary Krist, Kate Marsh, Marc Parry, Leslie Pietrzyk, Sarah Russo, and others in DC and beyond. My fellow ChickHacks are always an inspiration.

Abby Yochelson at the Library of Congress pointed me in the right direction, research-wise. The kind baristas at Peregrine Espresso kept me supplied with caffeine and general good vibes as I worked.

I am lucky to live in a city that values artists and writers. My literary life would be much poorer without the librarians of the DC Public Library and the fine booksellers at East City Bookshop, Politics & Prose, and the other top-flight indie bookstores of the DMV. The DC Council on the Arts and Humanities provided essential financial support with the award of a 2019-20 Individual Artist's Fellowship; that generous grant helped me see this project through its final stages.

I am grateful to my father, one of the most thoughtful and humane people I know, who taught me early on to love books, writing, and history; you'll always be my role model, Dad.

While my mother will never read this book, she helped shaped the person and the writer I am. I am grateful to her for that, for teaching me the enduring value of art, music, and nature, and for being such a devoted grandparent. My hope is that sharing some of what she went through will help other families who face similarly tough situations. You are not alone.

Lastly, I could not have written this book without the support of my family: my husband, Mark Trainer, and our children, Lela and Finn. Thank you for encouraging me at every step—and putting up with me through the process. You make it all worthwhile.